M000313459

MURIEL THE MEDICYCLE

Rick Carey

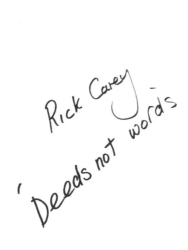

Rick Carey -

'Deeds not words

www.birlipress.com

Design by Euan Monaghan
Cover Design by Pro Graphics 360

ISBN (print): 978-0-6451631-2-4
ISBN (ebook): 978-0-6451631-4-8

Published by Birli Press 2021

I dedicate this book to my four sons.

To Craig Carey, Alex Carey, Ben Carey and Harrison Carey.

The most resilient men I know, all of whom lost their mother to disease whilst they were young men.

FOREWORD

In 2018, I bought a new Royal Enfield Pegasus motorcycle in the livery of the British Army Parachute Regiment; it was aptly named 'Peggy'. I have always said I would ride the BIG LAP of Australia solo and unsupported, and this seemed to be the opportunity. A friend said to me I should fundraise, so it was on.

A month later, I was touring the outback of Australia on a program called *A Bridge to Far*, in which I was raising funds for soldiers suffering with PTSD and enjoying time with many of the remote First Australian communities in the Far North.

During this mission, I became geographically embarrassed, i.e. LOST in the far north of Western Australia at a place called Wyndham. As I pulled into the town park, I noticed a group of locals gathered near a huge crocodile statue. I was out of water and food and very thirsty.

The group walked over and immediately asked if I was okay; it was a very hot day – 45 degrees, at least. There were old people, young people and children; they were so enthusiastic about Peggy and ultra-friendly to me. I soon sat down with them and enjoyed the cold beer they brought to me. I was accepted straight away.

The children loved Peggy and wanted to sit on her, tooting her horn, and sharing many giggles. One little girl wanted to play with my old Army whistle, blowing it with all her breath. Her mother, Muriel, introduced me to the family. I noticed straight away some had serious health issues, especially early onset of blindness, and one lady suffering from what looked to be leprosy. I was so shocked; I never knew this could exist in Australia, but I remembered it from my tour in Africa 1974-1975.

It gets dark early in WA. The evening moved on and I was enjoying the company of my new friends. All the men present gradually moved away, leaving me with a group of women (it felt like 'secret women's business'). We were soon sitting on the ground laughing and telling stories. Muriel sat next to me, and we all waxed lyrical for hours. In conversation, I told her I was very hungry. She quietly left the group with her aunty, leaving me on the ground talking.

Some time passed, and Muriel returned. She had cooked me damper and corned beef; I was so grateful. It was clear these great people had little, but what they had, they happily shared with a complete stranger.

Very late in the evening, we all lay on the ground and fell asleep in the extreme heat of Northern Kimberley. As the sun rose, which it does early, I found Muriel's head resting in slumber on my leg; it was a very human moment. I gently stroked her hair and woke her up as I needed to get up and head back to the turn off that I had missed the previous day. She and I walked to the local store for a coffee, leaving the other women looking after Peggy. They told me she would be very safe with them.

After some refreshments, I got ready for the road and said goodbye to Muriel and the girls. Leaving Wyndham was hard. I found myself thinking of the little girl who was so delightfully happy playing with my whistle. A sad thought entered my head: *Who has the courage to tell that little girl that she has little chance of a healthy life in this place?* I soon found myself weeping in my helmet and with a hollow feeling in my belly. It was not hunger this time!

It became sadly clear to me that these people are a forgotten people with little real help from successive governments. Their burden of disease is immense, with conditions like leprosy, syphilis, blindness, diabetes and so on very common.

It took a while, but from this experience my aspiration developed. I would return north in August 2019, delivering what care I could by way of basic medical care and First Aid. As a former highly experienced Combat Medic, I have spent a great deal of time working in remote areas with the

British Army. I started formulating a plan to use a modified Motorcycle Ambulance to gain access into some of these communities, offering a little help, and learning from them in return.

The mission was named *Muriel the Medicycle*, after the woman who inspired me with her kindness and generosity.

On my return from this odyssey, I put together a planning team, headed by my former Commanding Officer in the Royal Army Medical Corps. I was very keen to make this mission a success and I have always known PLANNING & PREPARATION PREVENTS PISS POOR PERFORMANCE. Originally, my objective was to raise funds through *GoFundMe* to buy a very capable motorcycle and equip it with comprehensive First Aid and medical supplies. However, it soon became clear that donations to the mission were not going to enable the purchase of a new motorcycle. My team suggested that I use Peggy again, as she was part of the reason I was accepted by First Nation communities. This was a deal maker for me, despite my own worries about her capabilities to complete another big journey loaded up to the gunnels. Equipping Peggy was easy. I modified her panniers, tyres, and crash bars, and purchased two Remote Area First Aid kits – all the time trying to avoid spending too much money by adapting and improving existing resources.

The team and I had several planning meetings at my home in the Snowy Mountains of Australia. We also took advantage of this, having campfires in my yard, partaking in good food, wine and single malt whiskey. These meetings turned out to be a valuable part of the mission's success.

We established five major goals in 2019 to facilitate assistance in communities in the Far North of Australia. These goals were not lofty and may have only scratched the surface of what is required, but a little help seemed better than the status quo. The opportunity to raise awareness of the challenges that First Nations people experience was a huge motivator.

DEEDS – NOT WORDS

1. To deliver First Aid and basic care to remote Indigenous communities.
2. To document and make photographic and other records of the social, health disadvantage and disease we encounter.
3. To bring these records and make them available to the media, politicians and the general community.
4. To deliver simple health and hygiene education to the communities we visit.
5. To provide some simple, fun and recreational programs in communities we visit.

During the year-long process of planning and adapting equipment, I experienced a great deal of self-doubt.

- Was I doing the right thing?
- Was I putting myself in danger?
- Am I capable of success?
- Will I be rejected?

- Will I make a fool of myself?

These fears were not helped by many of the reactions from some racist members of the public who viewed my Facebook page with derision and contempt, blaming First Nations people for their own predicament. I can honestly say I was frightened for my success, safety and reputation. I had to focus on telling myself to remain stalwart and tenacious, or I would have given up.

When I started this epic journey, I was ill informed, ignorant and somewhat ambivalent about the plight of First Australians. I was told that I needed to be careful and on my guard. Like many whitefellas, I had become flippant about the problems they faced. Once I reached the Far North of Australia, it soon became clear I had been sucked in by judgemental and racist attitudes. I found the blackfellas I met to be generous, friendly and very caring. The fact that their struggle was very real and yet they welcomed me with open arms made me feel quite guilty for being part of the problem, not the solution.

DAY 1

I'd decided very early on that the first day would be a short ride, making my first stop in Canberra, staying with great friends, Ken and Fran, before heading due north to Dubbo. I'm lucky enough to have a motorcycle escort: two local friends ride alongside. I enjoy the company as the highway can be boring.

On arrival in Canberra, I first visited my friend, Anthony, who lives in supported accommodation due to his disability. I have known Anthony for over 30 years through my community work with the YMCA and disability support. I want to catch up, as it has been some years since we last spoke.

The visit goes well, as Anthony loves motorcycles. He is thrilled with the prospect of our mission and to meet Peggy. We chat and laugh hard for an hour or so. Then I leave, telling him to come for a holiday at Bibbenluke soon. I ride to Ken and Fran's place with my escort.

On reaching Kambah, Ken and Fran are there to greet us. To my surprise, both my outriders know Ken and Fran very well; the motorcycle community in this region is very close. It is a good ice breaker because my introductions are comically unnecessary. After coffee, cake and conversation, my escorts leave, and I start to relax and enjoy the warmth of the sun beaming down on the deck in the backyard.

Later in the day, I enjoy a beer or two, but I am cognisant of my early start tomorrow and the need to start fresh. Fran is a great cook. I'd bought her a hi-tech pressure cooker for her birthday, so she cooks up some lamb shanks with fresh vegetables and mashed potatoes (one of my favourite meals), all washed down with a glass of red wine. Not long now, and I will be on my own. It may be several weeks, or even months, before I will be able to enjoy a lovely home-cooked meal like this again. In the meantime, roadhouses and my trusty gas stove will have to do.

After dinner, we watch some Netflix movies, retiring for an early night.

DAY 2

Upon waking, I can feel the itch to get going and make an effort to complete all my goals. Wish us luck – huge road trains await yet again!

Peggy and I leave Canberra, heading north towards Yass. The weather is clear, and the temperature is a balmy four degrees! I'm well prepared and rugged up in my thermals and waterproof motorcycle clothing, so I'm fairly comfortable in the bright sunlight. Once in the Yass valley, we enter a typical thick, freezing fog found in many of the low-lying 'frost hollows' that are common in this region in winter. This pretty much chills us very quickly. I hope it isn't going to be like this all the way to Dubbo.

We stop for a hot coffee and breakfast at the Yass service station. Fuelled up, we're ready to go further north, up the verdant Lachlan Valley. This area doesn't seem to be in a drought, as is much of NSW.

Part of the plan is to try and stop at each war memorial on route. The first is in Boorowa, which is dominated by its great arch and an old Vickers machine gun, the scourge of the trenches in WW1, killing millions of soldiers in the absurd efforts to charge and command enemy trenches across a muddy, bomb-cratered and wire-infested no man's land. 'Over the top' was the sergeant's cry; what a waste of young men's lives!

Then, on to Canowindra (pronounced Can-noun-dra). This town is famous for its very still air, and every year it is the focus for the International Hot Air Balloon Festival. Stopping at the cenotaph for photos, we are approached by a burly, kind gentleman in black motorcycle leathers. His name is Ivan, and he offers to take a photo of Peggy and me at the war memorial. He is terrible, Muriel, Ivan the Terrible, and very curious about Peggy and me. I thank him, give him our card and continue on through more emerald agricultural countryside.

Next stop is Cowra, a lovely old Australian town situated on the Lachlan River. Cowra was the site of Japanese internment and POW camps during WW2. Many hundreds of Japanese soldiers and interned civilians were locked away here in the heart of NSW.

It was also the site of the infamous 'Cowra Breakout' when Japanese POWs escaped captivity. The Cowra breakout occurred on 5 August 1944, when 1,104 Japanese prisoners of war attempted to escape. It was the largest prison escape of World War II, as well as one of the bloodiest: 545 Japanese

POWs escaped; the total number of deaths was 235. Peggy and I have to stop and record both the Australian and Japanese war graves.

The weather begins to warm up, and the sun shines on Peggy and me as we resume our journey towards Dubbo, NSW. We arrive in Wellington, 45 kilometres south of Dubbo; this seems like a good place to end the day.

Cheap pub accommodation is found in the Federal Hotel, just outside the city of Dubbo (and its many social problems). In short, it seems like a safe place to park Peggy for the night, so we pull in and book a room. I leave Peggy safe in a lockup car park and get settled in the early 1900s room with its small, single bed and green enamel cast iron sink. I would soon only be able to dream of having such a luxury. I go downstairs to the friendly, warm bar to write my daily blog for Facebook, whilst supping (an old Yorkshire term) on a schooner of Great Northern bitter – the start of things to come, no doubt. I do enjoy these old hotels and their Aussie atmosphere. Bangers and mash for dinner, a beer or two, and friendly locals showing an interest in Peggy and me.

Peggy performed very well today, despite all the equipment and survival gear she is carrying. I find riding her a little difficult at walking pace, but just fine at her top speed of 90 kilometres per hour. This makes me far more confident and happy. We have enjoyed today and it's just a short hop to Dubbo.

Being tired from the early morning chill and ride, I have an early night and will head for Brewarrina in the morning.

DAY 3

Getting up this morning, I have my last shower for what could turn out to be a few days, and dress, ready to leave. On going downstairs to the yard where Peggy is secured, I find she has a thick frost covering her saddle. It's pretty chilly!

I'm anticipating getting to Brewarrina. Having read Bruce Pascoe's book, *Dark Emu*, I'm looking forward to seeing the ancient fish traps used by the First Nations people to catch and kill fish for 30,000 years. I've also heard this town is a great model of success for Indigenous assimilation, whatever that means. Something my mind questions: *Why is our model of culture better than a culture that has survived 60,000 years?* Especially looking at how we are screwing up the planet. Anyway, I need to find out for myself, even though this is a significant detour on our journey.

Packing all Peggy's luggage and panniers, we are ready to leave. It's not long before we're on the road again, heading north to our first stop in Dubbo, NSW. No more fertile, green pastures in the mid-northwest of NSW: the paddocks are russet and parched. The drought has taken a great hold here. Heading into the Murray Darling Basin is thought-provoking, as I watch the skeletal cattle meandering around bone dry pasture looking for a patch of grass.

We stop for some quick refreshment and breakfast in Dubbo and to catch up with emails, messages and Facebook. Once hunger is no longer churning my stomach, we set off for the town of Narromine. I've fully intended to stop at the renowned Aeronautical Museum, so we do.

What a treat this place is to anyone interested in aircraft! Many aerial artifacts stand in a terrific display hangar, which includes a fully restored Rolls Royce Merlin Engine of Spitfire fame and a fully-functioning replica of the first ever powered flight, 'The Wright Flyer'. This reproduction has actually flown. We have quite a chat with the museum's curator. She is impressed with Peggy and our mission. We stop for some quick refreshment and breakfast in Dubbo and to catch up with emails, messages and Facebook.

After the aeronautical interlude, I'm back in the saddle heading north again in bright, clear weather towards Nyngan, the gateway to the outback, and apparently home of the bogan. We stop here to refuel and for lunch in a congenial cafe. After looking around many Australian towns, I am pleased to note that they often do their diggers proud, having a unique way of memorialising those lost. Nyngan is no different. It has a Huey helicopter on a towering display platform. This iconic chopper was responsible for many dangerous rescues and heroics during the Vietnam War, and it lives in the hearts of many old Aussie soldiers.

In the cafe, I speak with a farmer about the big dry. He says things are desperate, the water is gone and there's no rain on the horizon. This conversation proves to be a precursor for my own epiphany in regard to criminal water management in the northwest of NSW and increasingly Australia, in general. We have to start off again after lunch, but not before amusing the farmer's children with the balloon models from the kit I brought with me. The kids love it.

Our next objective is Coolabah, the turn off and refuelling spot before 150 kilometres of fairly remote, deserted road to Brewarrina. When we get there, it's a case of 'bugger!' The petrol station is now defunct and closed. Note to myself: *Never trust Google maps or local advice on the proximity of fuel.* Unfortunately, I have not yet filled my emergency fuel container. I am quite concerned that Peggy's range may not extend to 370 kilometres. Watching the fuel light like a hawk and avoiding any enthusiastic use of the throttle, we keep going nervously on a dead straight road, making plans to camp in the scrub bordering both sides.

The roads are lined with dead kangaroos and some pretty sick-looking live ones. I note a strange phenomenon of many shiny objects lying on the roadside. I stop for a closer look. I cannot believe my eyes – thousands and thousands of an introduced species, 'plasticus bottlus'! I do not understand why people would just discard so many in the bush. Obviously, these ugly items are thrown from cars to decay very slowly under the Australian sun. In a time when the issues of plastic pollution are so prevalent, it seems irreconcilable to me that people would do such a thing.

After an eternity, we finally make it to Brewarrina. My Gran used to say, "A watched kettle never boils!" I need not have worried – Peggy has four litres in reserve. That is an effective range of over 400 kilometres. Not bad for a little Royal Enfield Bullet, fully loaded with a fat, old, former digger and 80 kilograms of equipment.

After filling up with fuel, we head off to find our campsite by the river in an Indigenous-owned caravan park. I find my plot at the back of the well cared for park and set up my tent, sleeping mat and bag. It's now time to get something to eat and drink. I've been told the local club is a good spot and it is the town's RSL club. The club is patronised by many well-dressed blackfellas. I could have been in any RSL club in Sydney; only the shades of skin tone made it any different. Brewarrina seems to have adapted to whitefella culture. I'm quickly enjoying an ale in a town with an 80% Indigenous population and the food is excellent.

It's time to return to camp, so I go outside to Peggy and ride back to the caravan park. I go to warm myself by a campfire hosted by the manager. There, I meet a South African gentleman and very keen bush walker. We talk of adventures in the bush and his walks. Then, he gives me some advice on the selection and cooking of food, going as far as giving me a dried meal and showing me the stove he uses. We share anecdotes about equipment and survival skills before I give my apologies and head to my tent for some sleep.

DAY 4

After a long, uncomfortable, and cold night at Brewarrina Caravan Park, I rise early to get my old joints moving again. Lying on the ground is becoming less fun these days. I make my way to the local service station for coffee and breakfast, where I meet an Indian man who is extremely interested in Peggy. Of course, the Royal Enfield Bullet is made in India and the stuff of legend on the subcontinent. I ride back to my camp in the caravan park for a quick clean up and brush of my toothy pegs, which always makes me feel human again.

I really want to have an extended look around this thriving blackfella community and visit some of the local attractions. Brewarrina was not always mainly Indigenous in the past few hundred years. There was a mission nearby, 15 kilometres away. Believe it or not, until comparatively recently, Indigenous people had to ask permission to enter the town from their camp in the mission and were only first allowed to live in the township during the 1970s. A local tells me, "Our people were humiliated. It was like the Klu Klux Klan (ran the town)." The First Nations people received summary punishment for entering the township! That's within my lifetime – I joined the British Army in 1970 – and this makes me angry, frustrated and sad, all at once.

Whilst here, I have to visit the famous fish traps of the local First Nations people. These structures are over 30,000 years old, and some say the oldest, largest, man-made structure on the planet. They were carefully designed to direct fish into large holding pens, where they could be easily speared. I've seen old photos of this. However, the fish (in what is left of the Darling River) are a shadow of their former selves, as is the river, which, since European water management took control of the waterway, has collapsed – as we all know. Once upon a time, Murray Cod weighing up to 80 kilograms, and well over one and a half metres, were caught here. Nowadays, 28 kilograms is regarded as a huge catch. The structure of the traps is still clear, but much has been destroyed and allowed to disappear. In keeping with much of their architecture and structures in Australia, the true history of First Nations people has been bulldozed and removed from the records.

The local people are very warm and friendly, and keen to know about Peggy and me. During the trip so far, I've met several whitefellas who often say, "The government throws loads of our money at Indigenous issues and they still can't get it together."

Well, this community has, at least by our standards. Anyway, in my experience, when governments throw big bucks at a problem, they first set up a QUANGO (Quasi Autonomous Non Governmental Organization), or nefarious administering body. These bodies suck the system dry with bureaucrats, red tape and regulations. In the end, there is little funding left for the people who really need it. This is happening now also with the NDIS (National Disability Insurance Scheme), something I have experienced and seen for myself, while working in the disability sector.

I want to end today's story on a positive note. Go to the north-west of NSW, visit Brewarrina and enjoy its people and warmth for yourself. It's in a huge drought at the moment, but everyone has a 'can-do' attitude.

DAY 5

I wake early in Brewarrina this morning. It's very cold and frosty. It's funny how sometimes my Black Dog (depression) affects me in the morning. The paradox is all you want to do is sleep, but sleep can be a frustrating mistress and evades me. Self-doubt says, *'What the fuck are you doing, old man?'* I have to get up, get going and focus on my mission – pack up, rev up, and get on the road. Today, we will head off to the 'The Back O' Bourke'.

I meet with someone at the local roadhouse, a First Nations Elder who owns the caravan park. He questions me on my mission. He makes it all worthwhile, accepting and encouraging me to go on, even offering me a free campsite on my return. Suddenly, I'm fine.

After a bacon roll, a coffee and a short walk to loosen up, we pack up camp and are on our way to Bourke, and eventually Cunnamulla. The road to Bourke heads due west and the scrub is an absolutely arid expanse of dirt and weeds. It's only one hundred kilometres and we are soon in Bourke. We stop at a lovely little cafe shaded by small, green trees for our second coffee for the day. Peggy causes quite a stir with the little children looking at her. I make the babies some balloon animals. They and their mummies are really thrilled. This interaction is becoming a great motivator for me. *At this early stage, I do not yet realise just how much joy it would bring in remote, deprived communities.* My time here is a lovely interlude, but we need to head off, due north, straight into the blinding sun towards Queensland.

As we leave Bourke over a big bridge on the Darling River, we stop for a look and to take photos. I am shocked. The river is nauseating, full of blue green algae, it is just a series of filthy water holes and a sad example of what human greed can do to a once proud waterway. Dead birds, such as pelicans and cormorants, float on its acrid, slimy surface. I can only presume they have landed in this scandalous mess and been poisoned.

On the road north there is a cute little roadhouse at a remote spot called Enngonia. We stop for an ale, and chat with the locals. The locality is really a ghost town. The little school that lies opposite is derelict – just another bush community lost to lack of funding and government support. It's a short hop from here to the border, so I mount up and get going.

The scrub and desert are unproductive and parched, stretching out for as far as the eye can see. The narrow road is lined with roadkill that was obviously feeding on the grass on the verges. Kite hawks feed on the rotting carrion. They are quite a hazard as they lift off just as you approach. Hitting one of these scavengers on Peggy would not end well. Despite the bitumen road, it is a lonely place. We see only a handful of cars for hundreds of kilometres. At the border between NSW and Queensland, we stop at a small ramshackle outback roadhouse. It's the Aussie version of a motorway service area in Europe and so typical of the desert, with a dusty forecourt and shabby looking dogs sniffing around in the dirt.

As we near Cunnamulla, miles of new dog-proof fences border the roads and the scenery greens up a little; this area actually had heavy rains in Autumn. Spying along the roadside for a likely scrub camp for tonight, we see a good spot with a covered awning and BBQ area. However, first we go into town for a meal and a drink, returning at dusk when we are less likely to be noticed as I set up camp in the dark. The town is very tidy and well-managed. Groomed verges and monuments run down the main street which is dominated by an enchanting roundabout. In a local cafe that is just closing, a gentleman recommends a restaurant for dinner. I decide it would be just right and set off to find it. Cunnamulla has many long streets in an intricate spider web fanning out from the centre, so it takes a little time to find the place described to me. I eventually find it and park Peggy out the front. The establishment is modern, clean and tidy, but as the kitchen opens at 6.00pm, I have time to write up my daily blog and enjoy a cleansing ale. The food and the atmosphere in this place are equally outstanding.

The evening draws in. As light starts to fade, I leave, returning to the campsite I saw earlier. I set up my mosquito net and swag on the concrete underneath the tin awning, crawl in and wait for the great boon of sleep's oblivion to creep up on me.

All in all, we had a good run today, well over 400 kilometres, but no more night riding. It is very dangerous, as I found out last year in Kakadu where the road is a place where water buffalo and other wildlife wander as the air cools, making the bitumen a dangerous place for a motorcycle.

DAY 6

We rise to a spectacular sunrise; the rays of light were penetrating the tree line like shafts of gold this morning in Cunnamulla. Not a bad night 'on the tiles', despite the unforgiving cold concrete slab. Once we struck camp underneath the big awning, we set about getting packed and ready to leave.

Cunnamulla is such a warm, friendly place to find while heading towards the Red Centre, so breakfast in town comes first. Yesterday, I saw a sign advertising camel burgers. I was hooked – I just have to have one! Now, we seek out the establishment in this exceptionally neat Queensland town. We stop and order a camel burger, and it is delicious, tasting akin to really good wagyu beef. The hump, however, is very chewy! The coffee is the best I have had so far. I ask the owner where they source the camel, and she tells me about the local camel farm. Apparently, they castrate the male camels by bashing two bricks together on the testicles. I am shocked by such cruelty and ask, "Doesn't that hurt?"

She replied, "Only if you get your fingers caught between the bricks."

Boom-boom! (It's the way I tell 'em!)

On from here, we continue due north towards Charleville on the desolate Matilda Way. Again, there are very few vehicles, which is good, but it can become a tad monotonous listening to Peggy's 500cc thumper and staring at the vanishing point.

Another one hundred kilometres or so found us in a tiny outback locality called Wyandra, with just a few neglected weatherboard dwellings, post office and a pub. However, it does have a great tribute to all the fallen diggers in both world wars. This small, baking, dry place gave three of its own in WW1. That would have been a significant number of its manhood gone, but they're not forgotten. I have a coffee at the quaint historic post office, where they inform me they have a Facebook page called *Wyandra Post*. So, I look it up, as it's well worth the time.

After a little chinwag and exchange of information, we continue on to Charleville. The road is bound by never-ending spinifex grass. Pretty wild country if you were lost and 'dry as a nun's nasty'. The mulga trees appear like dehydrated skeletons everywhere.

We approach a place called Angellala Bridge, where there is an impressive memorial commemorating a spectacular event on this highway. In 2014, a truck loaded with 53 tonnes of ammonium nitrate caught fire on the bridge and exploded. The blast radius was over a kilometre in diameter, completely destroying the bridge, a railway bridge next to it and every emergency vehicle in attendance. For those who don't know, ammonium nitrate is the important ingredient in AMPHO, a powerful high explosive. The resulting shock wave was felt over 30 kilometres away. This was the largest transport related explosion in Australian history. Amazingly, no-one was killed, but eight people, including the driver, were seriously injured. A lot of religious meaning was made of the fact that one page of the driver's bible survived the inferno. Personally, I would have made a lot more of the fact that 99.9% of the text was incinerated, but that's just me. I will allow my readers to view the interpretive signs and form their own thoughts. But one thing is for sure, that would have been one big bang!

I sit in the lovely Charleville RSL club surrounded by some very impressive historical memorabilia including the propeller from a Spitfire, rehydrating myself before a further journey north and another camp in the scrub somewhere. I am surprised by the number of roadside placards objecting to proposed mining and fracking of this region, but then I remember they are totally dependent on the Great Artesian Basin for their water and their objections become clear. You can't drink contaminated water or money.

Peggy and I leave Charleville and camp in Augathella, a historic outback Queensland town famous for its meat ants. Yes! Ants that eat meat, and given the chance, they would eat you! Stockmen often place the carcass of dead cattle on top of a nest and within a few weeks it is picked to the bone; recycling of the fleshy kind.

We have dinner at a small hotel which is lovely, then retire to our little camp by the completely dry Warrego River. It was not always that way. In the bar, there are photos of locals drinking beer on bar stools with water way past their knees. Only in Australia!

It is pleasantly warm for a change. Some children are interested in Peggy and her mission, so I make them some balloon animals and chat with their father who is a doctor. He is keen to hear about *Muriel the Medicycle* and is impressed with our mission.

Eventually, I retire to my mosquito net and sleeping bag. Augathella is a pleasant place; the people are friendly and the idyllic camping by the river for Peggy and me costs only five dollars, which is placed in an honesty box.

DAY 7

In the morning, I wake at 0600 and decide to go for a walk to get moving and visit the local public loo. This gives me the opportunity to have a further look around this riverside town. I return to strike camp. After a week on the road, I'm getting good at it; I'm ready to leave in minutes. We ride back through the steep crest of the main street to the highway. I have a small breakfast in the roadhouse, where a beautiful girl from Chile serves me the biggest coffee I have ever seen and a greasy bacon and egg muffin. The balloon-modelling pump comes out. I make her a parrot in a swing model, for she has the most engaging smile and manner.

Time to go. Our first stop is Tambo and I have my first encounter on this trip with an over-taking road train. It's a small one, only three trailers and 53 metres long, but when you are on a little 'motor-sickle' doing 80 and the behemoth is cruising at 110, it takes lots of concentration whilst slowing (even further to let it pass), and then a wave to the driver to let him know his last trailer has passed. We reach Tambo after some 60 minutes.

Tambo is a very small place on this long highway, but still has a war memorial in the form of a trailer-mounted Bofors Anti-Aircraft gun. We head to the service station where I fill Peggy's petrol tank and have a coffee. Apparently, the town is famous for its teddy bears – they are everywhere. There's even a little shop with many furry friends in the window. However, I have no room for a passenger, so we take off, back on the road again.

On to another outback town called Blackall, home of the famous phrase, 'Beyond the Black Stump', legendary in Australia, meaning you are really in the outback. It's really just a very old surveying marker which was used when mapping of Australia started. The original rotted away and was replaced by a petrified tree.

Visiting the town's cenotaph, I'm privileged to stand by the statue of Lieutenant Towner, Victoria Cross and Military Medal recipient – a brave man, indeed. I stand to attention and salute, paying my simple respect. Blackall receives all of its water by bore from the Great Artesian Basin, an underground source. The water in the hotel toilet is typically sulphurous to smell; I've experienced this before on the Nullarbor last year. Should further mining in the Galilee Basin take place, this aquifer could be at serious risk of becoming toxic. I have with me a t-shirt sold to a friend by the traditional owners, the Wangan and Jagalingou people, and I wear it to show my sympathy for the plight of these people who are battling to prevent Adani from mining this country.

We go to the servo to fill up and encounter some dreaded Grey Nomads, a Mr 'Frank Incredits' and his mate, Mrs 'Deeming Rate'! They fill their huge $200,000 RV at the diesel pump, and then proceed to clean their caravan inside and out whilst at the PUMPS! Completely oblivious to people waiting to fill up! Ten minutes later, with Peggy and me sitting, waiting and overheating, they decide to leave, but not before arrogantly giving me a grilling about Peggy and her mission. They make cynical comments about how many resources First Australians already receive, comments I am sadly used to hearing. I don't think they like the Aboriginal flags we displayed. Anyhow, my generation can be cranky old coots, but Peggy and I are polite, and take off for Barcaldine.

After a long stretch of rather amorphous road, bordered by grasslands and acacias for as far as the eye can see (billiard-table flat, like many of Australia's continental flood plains), we arrive in Barcaldine. We need to fill up again. We ride through this organised town in the middle of nowhere and find a delightful war memorial – a huge comet wind pump used to drag water from the well years ago and the bizarre looking tree called 'The Tree of Knowledge'. It is protected from the fierce sun by a large shade structure. Because the area beneath the Tree of Knowledge was the scene of actions and decisions, which had a profound effect on the future of labour and politics in Australia, it has become an icon of the Labor Party and Trades Unions.

It is also important to the people of Barcaldine as a symbol of the town's identity and historical importance. This is reflected by the name chosen for the commemoration committee formed in 1987, the Tree of Knowledge Development Committee, and by the care given to the tree. In 1990, it was discovered that the tree was infested by termites and other insects and had severe health problems. Treatment by a tree surgeon, pest control and flushing of the root system with thousands of litres of water gave the tree a new lease of life. This treatment was completed in late 1993, but in 2006 someone gave it a thorough glyphosate drenching (allegedly 30 litres – someone meant business!) So, now it stands like a bleached skeleton in the town centre.

Only 106 kilometres from here through more flat native grasslands and onto Longreach, but not before we passed through Ilfracombe. A splendid place, its long main thoroughfare is lined with all manner of large plant, engineering and agricultural machinery from the age of steam to modern times. I take some photos of the more impressive iron leviathans.

Longreach, the home of Qantas, is only 27 kilometres from here. Peggy and I continue west. As we approach the outer suburbs of Longreach, my eyes are captivated by the superb roadside exhibits of a 747 (Jumbo Jet) and a charming vintage Constellation (Connie). The sight of these aircraft at the roadside in central Australia is a strange one indeed. I start looking for a campsite off the road, finding what looks like a dumping ground for building waste. It's perfect – out of sight, flat ground. It's a little early to set up the camp, so I ride into town down the long, wide main street, finding a hotel where I can have dinner and a drink.

My priorities are changing as we travel. Even on reaching our goal in the Kimberley, the reality is we will only scratch the surface of the problem. However, the further we travel, the more people seem to be getting on board. This is a great motivator for me; there is so much opportunity for sharing and raising awareness of the issues of life for Indigenous Australians and their children in the Kimberley.

I hope all those empathetic individuals keep sharing, keep talking, keep reading. Remember – the Kimberley does not have the highest suicide rate in the WORLD for no reason!

DAY 8

We wake up very early to a lovely, instantly warming sunrise that you can only see in the outback of Australia. We strike our little camp in the dump and go into Longreach for breakfast at a roadhouse, but not before saying goodbye to Dakota, Jumbo and Connie, the old airborne princesses. I just have to have a closer look.

After breakfast, I ask the girl serving me if they had a truckies' shower. It is common in the outback for the roadhouses to offer such amenities. This is my first shower and change of clothes in eight days. I am stinking! I really enjoy this simple pleasure, something we take for granted these days. I also took the opportunity to do some roadside maintenance on Peggy, adjusting her chain tension and lubricating a vital part of her transmission.

We eventually head off to Winton, home of the dinosaur in Australia. Many complete dinosaur fossils, such as the Muttaburrasaurus, were first discovered here and it continues to provide new evidence of reptilian life in prehistoric times. As we drive into Winton, I note this town exists in such a flat desert that its suburbs just spread out for miles; it's a small population, but an immense area. Winton is built in a classic grid structure; all the streets run parallel and long, so it's hard to find the centre.

Riding around in confusion looking for refreshment, we happen to bump into one of Peggy's cousins, a Royal Enfield Desert Storm 500. Like Peggy, she is ridden by an older man, tall, grey and looking as if he has been on the road for weeks. His bike is loaded up much like Peggy, but with less attention to detail (saddlebags hang precariously over the back wheel). We, of course, instantly get chatting and proudly waxing lyrical about our bikes and journey. We talk and decide to have lunch together in town. We find a clean, little cafe in the visitors' centre. I park across the road, but my new mate is less keen and afraid of the parking inspectors. My oppositional defiance disorder will have none of this and I park Peggy where I want! I think he is a little perplexed by my attitude. After lunch and coffee in Winton, we decide to ride together to Mount Isa. My friend is very firm on not going faster than 80 kilometres an hour, and sits exactly on that speed, not wavering one little bit.

The roads are so unswerving and tedious – nothing but grass and spinifex broken by the very rare road train or grey nomad overtaking. I only see about five other cars in 500 kilometres. Alongside the road are the odd crooked, strange posts, like bent long arms sticking up from the ground; on top is a glass insulator. I realise these are the remains of the overland telegraph, with dangling, long dead wires that once carried messages to loved ones across this boundless continent.

We are now in Kynuna. The Blue Heeler Roadhouse is a very hospitable and historic place. It reminds me of a hotel from a spaghetti western with its rails and veranda. Serving us is a personable young girl from Chile, and her friend. We hit it off straight away with this gregarious pair, so I make her a parrot in a swing balloon model and her male friend gets a green sword.

After a couple of beers and some dinner, we decide to ride a little further up the road to look for an appropriate campsite for the night. We find an old roadside gravel pit used by road train drivers for a rest spot about 30 kilometres from Kynuna. Setting up our camp in the grass, we both get our heads down for the night.

DAY 9

We wake this morning with stars still in the sky and the Milky Way showing the Dark Emu. I get up for my morning ablutions and greet my new-found friend.

The roads in the central west are very wearisome, going straight through barren prairies for hundreds of kilometres – not exciting like the twisting mountain roads and rainforest near my home. I am pretty much over them, but I have to stay alert for passing Multi-Axled Monsters. A smallish one pulls in just as we were leaving; only three trailers, but they get far bigger, so imagine that! When they are coming towards you at one hundred kilometres per hour, they remind me of those old snake toys with wooden segments swaying to and fro. That is what they do. Each trailer seems independent of the rest, and sometimes the last one oscillates side to side. It feels like it may just swing out, swiping you from the road, like swatting a fly.

So, we both get packed and leave our temporary home in the outback. At this stage, I am a little more concerned for my new mate as his load does not look terribly secure and he intends to go across the desert later in his trip. We head for a locality called Mt McKinley. There is not much here, just an automated fuel stop for trucks and 4x4s. However, we stop, and he kindly makes me a brew and a little tucker.

This isolated place does have quite a claim to fame. Its ramshackle pub is the very one used in the movie, *Crocodile Dundee*, in the outback pub scene and it hasn't changed one bit in 30 odd years. I go for a visit to the pit-dunny across the road. Walking across the ground is precarious as it is dried, cracked and broken like softened crocodile skin. My boots twist and turn as I walk. There must have been a flood at some time, but now it's baked crisp and brittle. Duty done and teeth brushed, we hit the road for the 120 kilometres to Cloncurry.

As we approach the birthplace of the Royal Flying Doctor Service, we are finally out of the tedious, bland badlands of the central west of Queensland. The terrain changes to rugged russet canyons, primordial rocks pushed up in some enormous geological event hundreds of millions of years ago. We reach Cloncurry and I just have to have a huge coffee and a pie at the bakery. I went there last year, and it is worth the stop.

Filling up with fuel because my riding companion is on reserve, I overfill my tank and the heat expands it. Fuel comes running out the overflow all over the road opposite the bakery. Note to self: *Avoid overfilling in the heat!* This often happens, but my friend is quite concerned and seems surprised at my casual reaction. All hunger pains gone, I leave Cloncurry – minus friend, as he wants to look around. We will meet up later, outside Mount Isa.

I love this type of country. Being a rock climber, I love looking at the possibilities of climbing routes and the dangers of massive rock fall in some of the many man-made road cuttings through this prehistoric landscape. On the way, Peggy and I pass the Burke and Wills monument. These explorers passed this way on their fatal journey in the 1800s to traverse the Red Centre and were never seen again.

Upon reaching Mt Isa, the first thing you see is the colossal mine dominating the whole town, with its waste tailings and tall chimneys pouring out smoke, visible 30 miles away. It seems incongruous to me that we live on such a breathtaking continent yet treat the environment with such contempt.

I ride into Super Cheap Auto to get a fuel bladder for the next 3,000 kilometres, as the distances between fuel stops may well exceed Peggy's range. I also buy some fresh engine oil; I need to do a service tomorrow at the roadside.

I sit in the RSL, enjoying a coldie and contemplating finding somewhere safe to pitch camp tonight by these busy mining roads. I am aggressively approached by an Irishman who questions me on my uniform and beret. He seems distressed and angry, telling me to take it off. Everyone is wearing hats, so I leave it on. He stomps off. I think his objection is as a result of what the Irish call 'The Troubles' and he simply does not like the British Army.

Leaving the RSL club, I start heading west again. After 60 kilometres or so, I find a perfect roadside camp near the remains of the old military-built road from the Second World War. We pull in and find shelter. Time in hand, I give Peggy a minor service, filter and oil change. I set up my camp and cook myself some dinner as the sun sets and its golden veil slowly fades to darkness.

So many huge road trains back and forth from the mine, there's no escaping the noise – the ground rumbles like an earthquake aftershock as each flies by. Eventually, my mind becomes accustomed to the rattle and din. I'm a little concerned one might leave the road and roll inexorably down the slope onto my little shangri la, but at long last sleep's darkness of mind follows.

DAY 10

Peggy and I rise to the never-ending sound of leviathans on wheels passing our little camp. I want to see the sunrise, as can only be witnessed in the Aussie outback, and I'm not disappointed. One can see where the First Nations Flag gained its inspiration. This campsite is a little memorial to those who pioneered this road during WW2 and I'm standing on a small, withered section of it. The interpretive signs tell the story of the courageous men and women who pushed this road through in what were then extreme conditions. The road was a very important part of the war effort, as well as getting troops and equipment to the far north as quickly as possible.

After the short history lesson, a visit to the dunny and back to camp and brew up. Good old Robert Timms' coffee and the ubiquitous sweetened condensed milk with which I became so familiar during my Army service; we used to suck it straight from the tube for an instant energy hit when cold or hungry. As I'm brewing up, my Winton mate pulls up. I can hear and recognise the rhythm of a Royal Enfield Bullet anywhere. He had camped further back towards Mount Isa in a truck stop and regretted it. We share coffee and I begin to strike camp, packing Peggy for the next part of our trip to Camooweal and the border with the Northern Territory. That will be three states now crossed.

He wants to stay to cook some porridge and check out the history, so we agree to catch up at Camooweal, and Peggy and I leave. This part of the odyssey starts to get a little more remote and fuel stops are distant and the roads even more lonely.

During the run, traffic is light, apart from oncoming road trains and the odd Grey Nomad in their RV or 4x4 and caravan, towing their living room, bedroom, toilet, shower and Netflix telly with them – doing the BIG LAP and doing it tough! I make the decision that when I arrive in Camooweal, I will have a decent meal, fill my fuel bladder and buy some groceries for dinner tonight.

The inimitable termite mounds start to appear either side of the road, looking like some burnt red cemetery, nature's gravestones standing in silent witness to the ever-present heat and wind. Termite mounds are interesting. Their shapes change in various regions: tall, or short and rounded. The big ones are adaptive to their location as they are aerofoil shaped with their narrowest face to the hot sun. Thus, they point north and are sometimes called magnetic mounds because you can navigate by them.

On arrival in Camooweal, I do all my duties – fuel, water and food. Plus, I try to post some details, but the repeater stations in this part of Australia are few and far between, not offering the best NBN coverage… Bahahaha! I also meet some Indigenous children whilst photographing the cenotaph. They love the balloon models which are a great ice breaker that will hopefully serve me well as I get more remote in the Far North.

My Winton mate turns up again and we go for some amber nectar in the outback pub. He decides he is going to visit some local caves and will not be following me on towards Barkly Homestead and eventually the Three Ways – the turning point for north, south and east right in the centre of Oz. We say our goodbyes because he will take the desert road west from the Daly Waters region and I will be going the long way round.

So, with that, another farewell and a 140 kilometre leg to a campsite at the roadside for tonight. Last time I rode this way, I decided to ride nearly 300 kilometres to Barkly. That was a big mistake! I was caught driving in the dark, which, on any motorbike or car on these roads, is very hazardous because of the wildlife. As well, headlights of oncoming road trains dazzle you for up to 15 minutes, because the roads are so long and straight. The hot cross-winds are notorious and there are several signs warning drivers of the increased fuel consumption and risk of caravan roll over. I'm riding at an angle of lean normally reserved for corners. Peggy stays true, despite her enormous load.

I'm now in a camping spot and settled, writing this blog. I've had a coffee, and dinner tonight is a tin of braised steak and onions with baked beans. There will be plenty of venting CH_4 tonight, I think. Good job my friend is a hundred miles back!

All my Army mates will know what I mean when I say I've forgotten my 'utes', 'KFS' or 'diggers'. Necessity being the mother of invention, a self-made paper bark spoon is just as good. It is very windy here and the bush flies are determined to drive me more insane than I already am! So, it's goodnight from me! I bed down under my mosquito net and in my sleeping bag.

DAY 11

Peggy and I get up quite early. Again, it's very cool and the wind has a bite to it. I break out the old camping stove and make a nice, hot mug of coffee to get me going. It's about 0545. Now warmed, I lie down again in the swag and just relax as the sun slowly rises to the east. At about 0700, I get up and make a breakfast of baked beans and a little of the braised beef leftovers from dinner. It feels good to start the day with a hot meal. After another brew, I start striking camp. Not a bad little area this, no water and lots of litter, but off the road and only 170 kilometres or so to my next stop at the very welcoming Barkly Homestead.

When we eventually arrive two hours later, it's very busy, with loads of RVs and caravans all jockeying for position at the only fuel pumps for hundreds of kilometres. Fortunately, Peggy and I can quickly nip in and fill up in minutes, then get out of everyone's way. It's a little oasis of civilisation at Barkly, with expensive but reasonable food and an opportunity to use WIFI and upload the previous day's events. So, health food it is! A Chiko Roll (nice and greasy) slips down easily.

My techno penance done for the day, I brush my teeth using the nearby garden sprinkler, which is busy chattering away, to rinse my toothbrush and mouth. Peggy beckoned, *'Let's get out of here!'* I mount my trusty steed and we leave for Three Ways, some 200 kilometres west.

At this point, we are on the Stuart Highway that goes all the way to Darwin on the north coast and Adelaide to the south. At a short stop to fuel up again at the Three Ways and have a drink, I meet a group of guys riding Harleys who are very curious to hear about Peggy's adventures. I run into an old soldier, who is a former Jumpmaster and Parachute Trainer. He is very keen to talk about Peggy Pegasus and her Parachute Regimental heritage. We have much in common: *Utrinque Paratus, Mens Sana in Corpore Sano.*

Leaving Three Ways is the first time I've really been apprehensive about the mission, mainly due to some truckies warning me about violence and theft in the north. I must brush this off and get on with what I feel the need to do. After the next 60 or so kilometres north, I find another roadside campsite at a place called Attack Creek. I won't go into the details, but it was the scene of violence between Indigenous peoples and European explorers trying to push through to the north. Let's say it did not end well for the travellers. Just something else to fuel my irrational fears.

After pulling in and settling down, I again meet the Para, and his partner, and their cattle dog puppy. We again start talking about old times in the Army; soldiers do that. I put my mosquito net up and swag down. Soon, I set about cooking my evening meal of sliced kransky sausage and beans. It's yummy. Another traveller brings me the most delicious tortilla with avocado and cheese, saying, "The cook made this for you." So kind!

Now, I will bed down for the evening, so we can start early for a great desert place, Renner Springs.

DAY 12

0547 and I get up as the sun starts to poke its first rays above the horizon. The physics of thermodynamics apply, and soon a chilly desert wind picks up. On with the billy and caffeine, the first order of the day. Note to self: *Always put your glasses on, as toothpaste tastes like shit in coffee, and the two tubes are similar!* What a silly bunt! I get my breakfast on the go and it is quickly eaten. Now it's 0700 and about time I start to strike camp. So, we get going on the Stuart Highway, heading north to Renner Springs.

When we arrive there, I have a coffee and fuel up Peggy. Renner Springs is a popular oasis and roadhouse, with thousands of discarded hats decorating the ceiling and walls. I take this opportunity to have a shower and change out of stinky clothes before moving on with the goal of reaching the desert nightclub of Daly Waters for the night. It should be fun there; it's famous for beer, music, food and lovely Irish girls.

Going north on the Stuart Highway, I ride through a lonely town in the Red Centre called

Elliott. This town was the scene of a powerful ABC documentary on the poor health and living conditions of Aboriginals recently. It is avoided by many travelling the route, as it has a bad reputation for theft and anger. I stop to have lunch and fill up. I see several First Nations people hanging around the roadhouse, most looking deprived, if not poverty stricken. Some look very ill, but no one makes me feel threatened or at risk. The town behind the roadhouse is a series of shoddily maintained homes with lots of poorly looking dogs wandering around sniffing for a feed. The place is another example to me of the deprivation and squalid conditions these once proud people cope with every day. Saddened, I get on my way to Daly Waters, still some distance from here.

I arrive back in Daly Waters for the third time (including last year's trek). This spot has to be both the remote watering hole and the jewel of the highway through the Northern Territory. I park Peggy next to their war memorial, where a lovely Jacaranda tree provides shade from the heat. There are many excited children running around the well-worn, corrugated iron buildings. I entertain them with the ever popular balloon animals which they really love and keep coming back for more, once the originals have burst.

There is a building with quite a collection of vintage vehicles across the hot dusty road. I wander in and inspect some immaculate vintage motorcycles and famous cars. The people I met earlier have parked their van in the caravan park, so we sit together and enjoy conversation, food and a few beers.

The Grey Nomads are in full swing dancing to Tom Jones, Englebert Humperdink and a myriad of American country music, not really my cup of tea. I prefer music with a far less American culture, and the singers are no more country folk than the nomads dancing. Finally they finish their shenanigans by joining a line and doing the conga around the pub. It has a joint age of 3000 years by the time they finish! I'm invited in but, being a Cranky Baby Boomer, I refuse to hold the hips of Mr 'Frank Incredits', so it's time for me to retire.

I find a little place in the dirt opposite to throw down my swag and mosquito net. It's a difficult night's sleep. For some reason, I've hurt my neck and it keeps waking me up. Ah well, dem's da breaks sleeping rough!

DAY 13

On rising at sunup, the usual hunt for coffee and food is on – not hard at Daly Waters. Shock, horror! My worst nightmare – I've lost my wallet! I frantically search all my kit and run around the pub asking anyone if I left it on a table. I calm down and go back to Peggy, lifting up my gloves and helmet from the seat. There it is! PHEW! Lesson learned. That done, we get back on the road north heading for Katherine via Mataranka.

The road is bordered by nebulous scrub for thousands of kilometres. This area was dotted with many RAAF air bases during WW2, far enough inland to be safe from attack, but close enough to defend the north and Darwin. We stop at the Pink Panther pub in Larrimah and have a look at the old airplane petrol engines lying around, including what looks like a Rolls Royce Merlin, which was used in the Spitfire and numerous other aircraft for many years. I go into this unusual, pink shack and look around the bar with its myriad of old Aussie relics on display. But no one is home, so I get back onto the highway to Mataranka – and yet more fuel.

The town is famous for its hot springs and thermal pools which are about 29 degrees and have crystal clear water welling up from the Barkly Aquifer hundreds of feet underground. This water source is also under threat from fracking and many protest signs attest to the local anger. It also has a massive tribute to the termite mounds that abound in the region in the form of a four-metre-tall replica of a magnetic mound in the main street. We continue north on the Stuart Highway.

I have a light lunch at Maccas in Katherine and buy water and rations for tonight's camp by the road. Peggy and I take a left turn to Western Australia and the Kimberley. At this point, the nature of the journey ramps up a little. Although the road is bitumen, it cuts a swathe through some of the most remote and hostile arid land in Australia. Driving 30 kilometres or so, we find a roadside campsite, pretty basic but quiet with no Grey Nomads. So, we stop for the night.

After setting up our little camp, I take a walk off into the thick scrub and through an area that has recently burnt. These areas of Australia are still untouched by modern man. Make no mistake, if you went too far in and away from your camp with no compass or navigation skills, you would quickly become disoriented, and with no water, find yourself in serious trouble. In the Army we used to jokingly say if you went bush with a British Army Officer who had a map and compass, that would be the last seen of you both! Except for my fellow APTC officers, because they are just machines and highly competent. I find a termite mound recently knocked over with some of the little white borers struggling for their life in the burning sun, trying to get back underground as soon as they can.

Tonight will be much hotter as we are now far enough north to experience the tropical heat. Also, from now on, all the remote waterways are dangerous as they contain big saltwater crocodiles. It's an amazing thought – that these prehistoric reptiles are this far inland. There are warning signs at popular rivers and waterholes.

Canned braised beef and beans again tonight – mundane, but nutritious – and wastes so little fuel to warm it up. You may remember I told you I lost my knife, fork and spoon? Well, no worries, because I've a collection at home that I gathered over my 40 years teaching in the outdoors. It's the same on this trip. I take a walk around several campfires and, as expected, I find lost or discarded eating utensils.

We will have been travelling for 14 days tomorrow; our goal is less than 600 kilometres away. With each kilometre I travel, my mind wanders and plays tricks, telling me I am a fool and should not be out here doing this work. This mission will be more about 'winning hearts and minds' than about basic medical help. It's always been that way: find a niche, exploit it and be accepted. Awareness of the issues facing those Indigenous people living in the remote Kimberley is growing. And by following my journey, more people are learning the truth.

Tomorrow, the road starts to wind down some of the most spectacular rugged river canyons, gorges and valleys as we head for Timber Creek and the border near Kununurra.

DAY 14

I am writing this at 0554, whilst having my morning heart starter in the scrub of the Aussie outback. I have just watched a moon set on the western horizon. It was ethereal as it slowly turned orange and dropped out of view. If I had not known, I would have presumed it was a campfire in the distance flickering and glowing like a beacon in the darkness. No sooner had that happened, than the bush was plunged into a darkness like squid ink under the ocean. Minutes later, the sun rose over my back: 'Let there be light.' This morning has been the first I have woken to and not been so cold. All my old joints and Army injuries have not ached – maybe because of the Ibuprofen or maybe because of the warmth.

Striking camp and leaving for Timber Creek at about 0730, via the Victoria River region, I love seeing the landscape change very dramatically from flat scrub, to big, red, striated rock formations showing the epochs of time to all passers-by. Just spectacular! The road is a consistent flood zone. It's not a great idea to do this ride in the wet season, and then there are the big saltwater crocs that migrate here and lie in wait a year or so for a meal. Evidence of the thousands of cattle roaming free is there to be found bloated and dead at the roadside, having been hit overnight by a road train whose driver would not have even blinked. One beast had even become trapped by the flood and pushed under a storm drain, its grisly remains sticking up for all to see.

On the road, I bump into two gentlemen who have ridden postie bikes all the way from Newcastle in NSW and, like me, are destined for Kununurra. I stop to see if they are all okay, but they are just refuelling their bikes. We chat about our respective journeys, then I resume mine. We will meet again, no doubt, a little further on.

I stop and wait to get a photo as they zoom by at 70 kilometres an hour, even slower than Peggy, and enjoying every minute. I have a strange hankering for chocolate and coffee, so I stop at Victoria River to refuel and scratch this itch. The boys on their step-through postie bikes just keep going towards Timber Creek.

Leaving Victoria River, I can smell the tell-tale signs of an Aussie bushfire, an odour with which I became familiar in the ACT Fire Brigade. I notice many birds of prey circling in the sky above the miles of still smouldering ground. The birds are looking for a cooked lunch which lay on the scorched earth between many charcoal-blackened trees. It's indeed fortunate Peggy and I were not here yesterday because the road would have been very dangerous.

Now in Timber Creek, I'm looking at the first boab trees on this trip. I shall see many more. Australia was once attached to Madagascar and the evidence is clear; we are the only other country that has native boabs. Plate tectonics have seen continents drift apart and Gondwanaland is no more.

We reach Timber Creek about the same time as the gents on their little postie Hondas. They are having a break, allowing us to catch up. I approach them and introduce myself. They are doing the big lap to deliver a letter in Sydney. They have an Instagram page, 'Posty around OZ', and have covered 5,000 kilometres so far. By coincidence, a rather flash sports car pulls in. It has 'POSTY' on its registration plates, so we all stand by and take pictures. I think there must be a connection. But, no – just a fluke!

Introductions exchanged, I go to the pub for a tinnie or two and the postie riders depart for Kununurra, WA. Whilst sitting outside the Timber Creek Hotel, I meet some gregarious Indigenous children and I start performing like a goose, which is normal for me. They are very excited by my balloon modelling skills; many balloon animals later, they let me go for that beer.

Having amused the local children, partaken of a cleansing ale and done some shopping for rations this evening, Peggy and I set off west in 30 plus degrees temperature, heading about 60 kilometres down the Victoria Highway to tonight's bush camp. We pass the Bradshaw Bridge, which spans the crocodile-infested Victoria River onto one of the largest military training areas in Australia. The sign says: 'NO VEHICLES ON BRIDGE', but Peggy also suffers with Oppositional Defiance Disorder, so she convinces me to go across for photos. Sometimes, she is a very naughty sickle!

Continuing on, we find a great little spot at the roadside with water tanks and a covered table to cook on – luxury! Boab trees surround the camp. I can't resist the temptation to carve my corps badge… Now, there is a little symbol of our exclusive brotherhood in the Australian Outback!

Soon after getting set up, a little travelling family arrive. It's great to see parents exposing their young ones to the great Australian outback adventure. The father and I take his son to explore the scrub looking for the boab fruit, which we find. I also teach the little boy how to use the sun to navigate in thick bush and find his way back to his camper; it was a nice little interlude.

Whilst walking around the area, I notice a man-sized termite mound. So, I dress him up as another APTC Sergeant Instructor standing about with little to do. The dressing up of termite mounds is something you see a lot of in the far north. He provides me with his rank and name, 'SI Termite

Mound', and welcomes me to his gym in the wilderness.

Later in the evening, conditions are good, so I light the first campfire of the trip. It is nice to just sit and watch the flames, often known as the bush telly in Australia, dancing in the semi-light of a full moon.

The evening is somewhat marred by the presence of a large feral cat looking around for a feed. For my English friends and cat lovers, these wild felines decimate birds and small marsupials in Australia and are far from popular. As the moon rises high, it's time to hit the swag and get some well-earned sleep, despite the heat.

DAY 15

In the morning, I cook breakfast and coffee then strike camp, say cheerio to the family and head off west towards the Western Australian border. The vista is breathtaking, with the rising sun behind silhouetting and showing off the huge red rocks and cliffs. We pass thousands of Brahman cattle wandering around the outback paddocks, but never straying too far from their water supply.

As we approach the border, signs warn us about quarantine restrictions on fruit and other food-stuffs. The customs officer spends little time assessing that Peggy is not carrying any and quickly sees us on our way.

Next stop is Kununurra and the massive Ord River Dam and the irrigation system of Lake Argyle. In search of morning tea, we find a corner cafe and park outside. I visit the local camping store to buy a new camp mattress as the one I have is going flat overnight, not helping my older adult aches and pains. When I return, Peggy has attracted the attention of a journalist, who wants to hear all about our mission and says he will pass on our details to the media.

I take this opportunity to visit the laundromat with all my dirty clothes. This mundane task takes a while.

Finally, washing done, we leave Kununurra on the Great Northern Highway towards Wyndham, WA. Wyndham is as far as possible that we can go west because the road ends at the Port of Wyndham, which looks out over the Timor Sea. We're travelling the Kimberley proper now and it is unmistakable: massive, red sandstone canyons and burned, rocky landscapes are everywhere. We pass The Gibb River Road, an infamous route of 700 kilometres through the mountains to the coast at Derby. It destroys the cars and caravans of the unwary on a regular basis and can take weeks to get through if you have a mishap. There is only one rescue service about halfway and he is kept busy with fixing axles, tyres and transmissions.

We're approaching Wyndham on the newly-made road. Last year it was barely a dirt road, but the port is now going to be used to export mining produce, oil and gas to China. It remains to be seen if this helps the Indigenous people.

As we reach Wyndham, there is a bushfire with flocks of scavenging birds spiralling, diving and catching the frightened critters escaping the flames. I'm tired, and I stop at the '22 Metre Croc' in town to sit down and get a drink. A First Nations lady approaches me, wanting to sell me a beautifully carved boab nut; the people here carve native pictures on the shell with knives and sell them to tourists. I'm somewhat reluctant to buy the item so early, as I have nowhere to keep it safe. So, I make her a balloon model and she tells me a little about herself and her life in Wyndham. She is a sad figure: unhealthy, malnourished, few viable teeth and depressed. I feel great empathy for her. She also tells me Muriel, the lady who I met last year and whom I named the mission after, has moved to Port Headland with her little daughter.

When refreshed, I go to the small but expensive town shop and get some dinner to cook for tonight. All fresh food here is double the price of that in our big cities due to the remoteness.

Peggy and I then ride to the caravan park to establish what may be our home for a few weeks. We shall see. I'm hoping to gain some trust here and get some contacts that may help me deliver my intended goals throughout the Kimberley.

The caravan park is really well-maintained, with clean facilities and welcoming staff. I'm directed to the back of the park near a dry creek bed where I set up my little camp. I go over to the modern camp kitchen and prepare my dinner. By this time it's dark; it gets dark very early this far north.

In the evening I go to a bush camp gathering my new blackfella mates called 'The Pond'. It's a fairly rowdy affair so I fit in well. The Pond was at one time a large area of water, but it has been filled in by officials because it was a gathering place. Many of the community Elders are there, so this is my chance to develop some relationships and get to know locals. I am accepted by these great people who allow me to play games and interact with their children. After spending a couple of hours around the campfire in the dirt, I return to my camp and retire to my swag for the evening.

DAY 16

I should describe Wyndham and the Kimberley. The average annual day time temperature here is 36.5 degrees, with maximums near 50 degrees, so it's fair to say I am hot. Many early settlers died of heat stroke here. Wyndham is an old seaport with quite a history of exports, such as live cattle, processed meats, gold and iron ore. Now, with the mining of rare earth metals for batteries and so on, it may well become a major export centre again.

This morning is for getting to know the First Nations people living here. So, after an anxious night, Peggy and I rise to a very warm 22 degrees at 0500, as it gets light then. After a coffee and relaxing, I have a shower (luxury!), put on clean clothes for the first time in a week and go to cook a bacon roll for breakfast with yet more caffeine.

I prepare Peggy to go into town and meet more people. We ride around town a little, seeking out company. There is a group of women assembled nearby under the shade of a mulga tree. They recognise me from last night at The Pond, so I go over, and we start getting to know each other. I fit in well, perhaps from my experience working in remote Africa in the mid '70s. There, I was required to facilitate medical relief work to the tribal communities of Southern Sudan, a very valuable asset to me on this mission, giving me the skills to understand and be empathetic towards dispossessed people.

I never expected to be offering help this early in my mission, but a woman has a nasty, infected head wound above her right eye. I offer to fix it up and she happily lets me clean and dress it. The gash really requires about five sutures but is so old it would now require debriding and scrubbing before doing that, so I only offer first aid. I suggest that she go to a hospital.

Next, a dishevelled, unhealthy gentleman approaches me, limping. He complains of lesions on his lower leg and asks for antiseptic medication. I offer to look, but he refuses. Trust will come slowly, I think.

Another lady has no fingers on her left hand. I ask her what happened, and she says they had been cut off because of infection. That was possibly secondary to Hansen's Disease (leprosy), due to the neuropathy which causes a numbing of feeling due to nerve damage. Sometimes, people cannot feel when their hands get injured, and in this climate infection soon follows. I can do little to help her, except to say that I will be back tomorrow.

A rather extroverted man who I met last year, and who calls himself Mr Bean, has what is probably trachoma, as his eyes are very irritated and inflamed. I offer some soothing eye drops, which he is happy for me to administer. I give him a couple of days supply.

I do ask if I may record such things with photos. However, photography is difficult as cultural differences and an innate pride makes people dislike any formal record keeping, so you will have to take my word. Anyway, a Day One clinic is successful, and I tell everyone I will be around for at least ten days, so let's see where it goes. The young mother whom I met yesterday, tells me how her life was destroyed when DCP (Department of Child Protection) officers took her babies at birth! She was only 17 then, and she says she has never recovered from that trauma. This happened to her in the late nineties. Her children are now living thousands of kilometres away. She never sees them. So, for those who believe the Stolen Generation is over – wake up! It is happening to this day.

Another male Elder, who is very friendly, tells me of his enduring grief: his culture, land, language and opportunity have been buried, bulldozed and the true history of his people is ignored; we are now destroying his people's land for mining, water and profit, giving his people nothing in return. I truly feel his frustration and anger. Despite this, he is very kind and polite to me, and not the stereotypical, alcohol-damaged Aboriginal we have been brain-washed into seeing as the norm.

In the centre of town are some impressive 23-metre-tall bronze statues of the region's First Nations Warriors who lived in this land success-fully for over 60,000 years. With their weapons and hunting tools, they stand and look proudly to the hills overlooking Wyndham, along with some of the fauna they would have hunted for millennia. I'm so impressed by the power and pride the artwork conveys.

I decide to take a ride up to the Five Rivers look-out on the Bastion, a castle-like geological struc-ture perched high above Wyndham, to inspect the views. I'm not disappointed, gazing out over the five rivers that all converge at this point in the estu-ary to the Cambridge Gulf and East Timor Sea. These ancient deep, dark rivers are infested with massive crocodiles. There used to be a giant meat works here, where two million cattle met their end. It has a blood drain, a channel where all the offal and blood was pumped into the Cambridge Gulf, encouraging the presence of deadly reptiles and big sharks. I take photographs of Wyndham Port and its adjacent structures, and the blood drain where the meat works discharges into the gulf can be seen.

Returning to the town, I go to the place where people congregate during the day, at 'The Croco-dile'. The local people carve the most intricate art onto the fruit of the boab trees and sell them to tourists. As one Elder tells me, the money earned first feeds their babies and after that they may buy a few tinnies. I can't blame them – it's stifling here, and who complains when us whitefellas have a few quenching ales in 40 plus temps and high humidity?

After a busy day getting to know the Indigenous community and riding around looking for photo opportunities, I again spend the evening with two families around the campfire in the sand at 'The Pond'. Funnily, I'm baking hot after a 35 degree day, but as it drops to the mid-20s, my hosts say it's cold and their children ask for jumpers. With that, another toasty campfire is lit.

People here are friendly and accept the company of an old whitefella. They tell me of other communities that inhabit parts of the Kimberley, accessible on Peggy. One such place is called Warmun. The Elders give me contacts and introductions, so I think that may be our next stop. It's more remote and only has one roadhouse. It's a closed, alcohol-free area, so I expect the community will have far less than those here in Wyndham, which is a nicer place to live for some – mostly the whitefellas.

I am so happy I brought the balloon models – the children just love them. I'm trying to convince the blokes to play Oztag at some stage, but slowly, slowly does it. Finally, for the day, thanks go to Mr Bean, who gives me a carved boab nut and poses with Peggy for me.

Last year, I was taken aback by the level of extreme dental disease in this region. Well, that observation has only been confirmed this year – nearly ALL Indigenous adults here have advanced dental disease, unlike anything I saw as a combat medic in the South of Sudan. Only the smallest of the beautiful children have any viable teeth. Poor dental health is killing Australians here, for we now understand the links with heart and brain health. Dental blood circulation and nerves of the head and neck are directly associated with both these vital organs, so infection and inflammation spreads easily. I find this situation particularly emotional because I can do little to help. Governments of all persuasions are vicariously guilty of negligence, Indigenous disease and death over decades – there, I said it!

As for the Government's lies, propaganda and assertions that our Indigenous people abuse their children, I have seen no such thing – just love and affection, despite extreme living conditions. We must all now know that the Aboriginal 'Intervention' propagated in the Howard era was based on a lie, designed to get these ancient people off their land, so we can frack and mine the heart out of it. Don't believe me? Do some digging and you will find the Government Officials who came up with it, and recently the ABC exposed the scam.

DAY 17

I want to do a little tourist stuff this morning and find out more of the European history of this congenial place, so after some breakfast and coffee, Peggy and I set off to inspect historic Wyndham Port, a place with a busy past. I think it will again be a major export hub for mining, live exports and fracked gas, and so on.

First, we go to the Pioneer Cemetery where many graves of those who succumbed to the heat of this place (one of the hottest regions in Australia) are found. The graves all pre-date 1929, and the last person interred was Charles Bridge, a merchant and businessman in the region for many years. Many of the graves are unmarked, and because this plot is often inundated by the ocean at high tides, the settlers and workers had moved to a new site at Gully Cemetery. I note that at least two of the graves are managed and kept in good order by the Australian War Graves. I lay my beret there for a couple of minutes and take photos as a mark of respect, from a very old APTCI.

After a morbid stroll around a feature that fascinates me for some reason that eludes me, we ride up through the old port and photograph a number of pre-WW2 steam trains that transported goods to waiting ships, often bound for 'Blighty' with frozen corned beef on board. We stop at a little shop run by a local character. She's wearing a t-shirt that says, 'Grumpy Old Woman'. I comment that I am a Grumpy Old Man and we hit it off straight away with lots of self-deprecating banter and hearty laughter. Her little tin shop is an eclectic mix of bric-a-brac. She says she sells the stuff to passing tourists because no one in town really wants it.

There are two strange catfish skulls on display. No kidding! They have a bone structure that looks like Jesus on a crucifix and on the reverse, the devil. It really is uncanny! I don't like to ask for photos because she needs to sell them. We chat for 15 minutes or so about Wyndham and its celebrities like Mr Bean's brother who was a master boab nut carver, before Peggy and I go back to town for a meeting with my newfound friends.

I assist four people today with minor ailments. An adorable little girl has an infected wound on her foot, which I clean and dress. She also has a minor fungal infection (ringworm) on her chest. I advise her loving parents on how to treat it successfully, but I shall be buying in some antifungal ointment for her ASAP.

A gentleman has a sprained ankle, and his compression bandage is doing no good, so I remove it and reapply it more effectively. Another nice gentleman is in pain from a foot injury, so I give him some over the counter pain relief, enough for two days, telling him he could use it four times daily, if he liked. Of course, eye drops are popular here because of endemic trachoma or toxocara, so I again administer some soothing drops. Australia is the last developed nation on earth to still have trachoma infections in its population. We should all be appalled by that fact – it's blinding thousands of our people!

The rest of the morning, I spend at The Pond with a lovely family. Also, there are grandparents, but it is customary for the females to sit away because the mother-in-law cannot sit with her son-in-law, so the two groups never spoke. The grandad is an interesting man in his 70s who has a wealth of knowledge about the region and life of its people. I enjoyed learning from him about their lives, deaths and previous homes in Oombulgurri, a community not far away from which they were forcibly evicted just several years ago, and their homes were bulldozed to prevent return. There was also the Forrest River massacre of his people within living memory.

The children play in what is left of the pond which is still topped up by a hose connected to a standpipe. The youngest little girl is floating the white balloon swan I made for her. Her mum tells me she calls me 'Balloon' because she has not mastered Rick yet. Apparently, the pond used to be much bigger and full of barramundi, which locals caught and threw straight on fires. However, it seems this focal point is not popular with the 'fun' police because it was drained, leaving barely a puddle now filled by a hose which the wee one took great delight in playing with. The play is all dirt, water and mud pies, just like the days when I was a child, and the gathered people love and protect their kids as much as we do in our own culture.

The 36.9 degree temperature becomes too much for this old git from the Snowy River region of NSW, so I say, "See you after sunset," and go back to my base camp, where I escape the heat under the shade of the trees and light breeze in my mosquito net.

DAY 18

I am so happy that fate led me to this place. It's a small dry and hot place, but it has everything I need. I may be sleeping rough, but at least I can shower at the lovely little Wyndham Caravan Park, which is small but pleasant and a great base for me to move out and meet the true Aussies in this region. It has a water hole down the back, but don't go there in the wet season as there are crocs. A guest lost her arm and her dog years ago! To this day, dogs are always getting taken at the local jetty.

Sunday is a quiet day here. Even the grog shop is closed, which is a shame because I need a beer and it's only 10.13am, but 30 plus degrees already.

Peggy and I ride out to visit some historical landmarks this morning, namely the Muslim Afghan Cemetery, where the pioneer cameleers are buried facing Mecca, with their camels! Without the cameleers, this region would never have been developed as it is now; they used their camel trains to bring in vital supplies. However, there is much they did to local Aboriginals that I'm told was not so good.

They were also pretty much discriminated against; the cemetery is a burnt-out patch of land way out of the community. We also go to the main cemetery, which is still in use, a reflection of the townsfolk's respect for their dead. There are no crematoria here in the distant northwest.

Down the road a bit is the 'Work Camp', a correctional centre for troubled youth from all over the Kimberley. In my day, it would've been called a 'Borstal'. Incarcerated young men in Western Australia and the Northern Territory have been in the news recently. A place called the Don Dale Youth Detention Centre was exposed for the use of restraint chairs and other cruel treatments from the dark ages. I hope this place gives these young men and women some remote respite from the abuse they receive at the hands of governments, by giving them focus that takes away the anger about the injustice their people have endured for so long.

We all must live, so Peggy and I go to the little shop to buy some rations for the next few days. Of course, there's some bacon, beans, bacon, sausages, bacon, bread, bacon, milk, bacon, more First Aid supplies – and let's not forget the bacon! Hey! Bacon keeps in the heat! We meet some young lads in the shop and, of course, they want Mr Balloon to make balloon swords, which I do, and they start an enthusiastic fencing bout.

Back to camp to drop off the bacon and then a cruise around the now non-existent community.

Being Sunday there is no-one around at The Pond, so I go to another spot by the 'Big Crocodile'. There, I meet another artist who is carving a boab nut for passing tourists, and her friend, an interesting fella with strong knowledge of ANZAC, having served in the Australian Army for many years. He expresses strong feeling about his 'country' and how it has been exploited and raped by successive influences, corporations and administrations. He is not angry, just saddened and beaten. I'm not surprised because the country he served has abandoned him. We sit in the increasing heat for an hour or so, just chewing the fat – a good interaction.

After this, I get onto Peggy for a cruise around. It's still very quiet, so I think I will come back to base and do my 'dobie' or washing for all non-soldier types. I did it in the fashion used in 1970 when I joined as a boy soldier at 15 – by hand in the sink, or bathtub, if you had one.

Whilst it is soaking, I take time to write some more of today's blog, then I return and pummel the said 'dogs and shreddies' (terms soldiers use for their socks and underpants) until they no longer 'pen and ink'. Then, as my recruit corporal showed me, the low-tech spin dryer that takes ten seconds and uses only wrist power. For those who know me, I have loads of wrist power from excessive use of a motorcycle throttle.

After the Chinese laundry, Peggy and I take off in search of a war memorial here. We find one, but for some weird reason it's locked away behind a steel fence in Wyndham Port. It's a sad affair; I think it may have been vandalised. After paying our respects, we go down to the waterside for a paddle. I put a handkerchief with knots in each corner on my head and roll my pants up, much like the British do at the seaside. I'm about to go into the water when Peggy shouts, "Hey, TWAT! If you want to be a handbag's lunch, then keep going!" She has always had more smarts than me, so I quickly tippy-toe out of the bitey-critter mud bank.

Returning to town, Peggy and I visit the home of an Elder I met last night. The footy is on the telly and bores me to tears, so I get the kids and go for a ride on Peggy, breaking the law with these excited children by doing laps up and down their street with no helmets, and making silly balloon animals. The wee ones just love it. We have lost something in our big cities with all our rules and regulations. Life has risks – DEAL WITH IT!

I'm invited into the home by the Elders to watch the AFL Richmond vs West Coast Eagles and have Emu-piss tinnies thrown my way. Sometimes, you just gotta go with the flow, especially when the company is excellent people, and delightful, joyous and carefree children.

I am loving this adventure. Sometimes, the best thing you can do is to demonstrate love by just giving someone you'd never met before a band aid and some betadine. DEEDS – NOT WORDS!

DAY 19

A lazy lie-in this morning, then up to glorious sunshine and a native bird calling 'Richard! Richard!' I think it's my mum, so I rise to have breakfast and caffeine. SSS, for my Army mates who will understand. Then it's *on with the pixie hats and bring on the skating vicar*, as the Monty Python crew might say.

On the road today, Peggy reckons she can handle a rough dirt track for 60 kilometres into the desert to see the Aboriginal rock art in local caves and visit the infamous 'Prison Tree' I see mentioned on historical signs in Wyndham. So, we turn down the highly corrugated and rocky Kings River Road. Anyone who's driven corrugations knows you have to get up to speed to avoid getting shaken to pieces. Of course, that means you are pretty much floating across the roads, so there's no sudden turning or brakes.

When we get to the road's end, we've reached Moochalabra Dam, the source of Wyndham's water. It's 24 kilometres from town and is somewhat of a strange sight out of context with the surrounding deserts. Of course, there's no swimming. 'Be croc safe' is the saying.

We also stop to look at some ancient rock art I have seen promoted on some indistinct road signs, supposedly over 30,000 years old! It involves a short, but steep grovel up a rock ledge, so I don't think many Grey Nomads would get to see it. I'm exploring some of this astounding culture left by the oldest living civilisation on the planet. The art depicts the creatures, landscapes, rivers and people of the region and not a dot in sight. Being in its ancient presence is indeed a privilege. I see a large piece of rock looking like the ripples on sand at a beach or shallow foreshore, and that clearly demonstrates the marine origins of these old rocks from epochs past.

Afterwards, Peggy and I resume the dusty, rocky ride to visit the notorious Prison Tree, a huge hollow boab in the desert. Here, our First Nations people were incarcerated and tortured in chains inside the arboreal dock, suffering and dying for killing cattle, or the whitefellas who were invading their land. I climb inside and find it difficult to clamber through the small hole. Locals tell me as many as TEN blackfellas were squeezed into the small, hot space! It is incongruous that only a short distance away there is artwork painted by peaceful early man, depicting their home, animals and lives. Contrast that with our occupation – a vile dungeon with no escape, food or water! I ask you, who is the savage? Having seen this obscene hole in a tree, I can assure you it's not the First Australians, who were living here for many, many millennia.

With this going through my troubled mind, I mount faithful Peggy for the bumpy, dusty ride back to Wyndham. I sit down at the 'Crocodile' with a small group of Indigenous locals with whom I'm now familiar, and we enjoy a cold beer, just like any European might do. As we're sitting there, it's pointed out to me that we're being watched on police surveillance cameras placed on a big pole. I think this is a contemporary version of the Prison Tree, keeping modern blackfellas restrained in their own land.

I go to take a nanna nap, as my nerves are frayed by today.

DAY 20

Today was always going to be a slow one, as people are just starting to warm to my presence. So, after the usual ablutions, sausage and beans breakfast, Peggy and I go into the township and start making enquiries about the second goal of this mission.

We head to the small job centre, which directs us to the council office and their Recreation Officer, where I'm directed on again, but I'm not going to take 'no' for an answer. Eventually, I meet a young woman in a building with a covered roof over a basketball court. We have a constructive discussion about getting the local children involved in a game of OZTAG, which she has never seen. Oztag is played the same way as touch football or Rugby League, with one exception – it should be entirely non-contact. The idea is to affect a 'tackle' by grabbing coloured tags stuck to a belt around the waist of the players. If successful, it is regarded as an effective tackle and the team with the ball loses one of its six chances to score in the usual way. The tag is placed on the ground to signify where the tackle occurred, and play continues until six tags are made. So, tomorrow at 1400, we're meeting with local school kids to teach them to play the game and introduce Peggy to those who have not yet already met her.

After this success, we wander over to the meeting place by the 'Mega Crocodile' and sit, talking with Elders. One asks me if I could ride up the road and collect boab nuts for him to carve. They sell for up to $50 each, so good ones will bring in some much-needed cash. This I do. When I arrive at the spot, all the nuts I can find are damaged or in the trees. I decided to use the Gurkha Kukri knife my friend, Peter Macie, made for me and attack a fallen limb to make a stick to dislodge the nuts. It reminds me of scrumping apples as a little boy. In my efforts, I nearly chop off a finger in one big swing that ricochets off a twig. All to no avail, because all the nuts are damaged by the heat. But across the road is the town's lonely police station with a divvy van parked. The trees there look well-watered, so I went in and nicked some of Bobby's nuts, then scarper quickly on Peggy.

Successful, I get back to 'the Croc' and give my ill-gotten gains to my new mate, the artisan of the nut. Pleased with my gifts, he starts to carve. Sitting and waiting is not my strong point, so I leave to get some lunch. Later, some children come over and ask about Peggy. We make them some balloon models and talk all about the adventures of Peggy, the little green Army bike.

As the sun sets, Peggy and I go over to the camp at The Pond. There are many children there and they all want to have a ride on Peggy, so I have to oblige. It's such great fun listening to excited kids jostling and screaming in delight, whilst we go around and around the pond at about five kilometres an hour. It's all about perception, and children are a delight at such times.

Anyway, all good things must come to an end, despite the protests of giggling babes. Just as dark sets in, a flock of the filthiest cockatoos arrive to drink. It's comical watching these Charlie Chaplin raptors strutting around like pompous fat men.

I return to my camp and cook a meal.

DAY 21

I have a good night's sleep and dream of my lovely whippet puppy, Loretta, at home being cared for by my good friend, Anthony. They are nice dreams and, as I don't usually have nice dreams, a bonus to me. Lying on my sleeping mat underneath a mosquito net and waking to the dawn chorus of native songbirds is a pleasure, for once. I cook a greasy bacon buttie and coffee for a healthy breakfast; funny how I never tire of bacon – must be a male thing. Bacon trees are a great resource!

I wake Peggy up and kick her in the guts. She chugs into life straight away, then we go into the little cafe in Wyndham, just for a second brewed coffee, before starting out to the museum in the port. We look around outside this rather run-down building, but there are some wonderful artefacts from early last century. Of interest to me is a hot/ cold piston engine. A wood fire heats air in one chamber, which expands and drives the piston upwards pushing a flywheel. The hot air then goes into a cold chamber and as the air cools rapidly, it contracts, sucking the other piston down and providing further energy to the flywheel. We truly are an innovative lot, we Homo Sapiens. What a shame we ignore the realities of all our impacts on the planet and its interconnected matrix of life. Ho hum!

There is also a display about two German Aviators in 1932 whose plane crashed in the remotest part of the Kimberley and how they survived 40 days on their wits and a makeshift canoe. As if that was not enough, recently a young chap, re-enacted the whole survival story for his own amusement. Truly! It makes for a very impressive tale of ingenuity and tenacity of the human spirit.

We also meet a young man who is in the area tending Aussie Diggers war graves. Here is so remote, but Australia honours its soldiers, no matter where. He is responsible for all war graves in an area bigger than Great Britain. He is with his lovely little family so of course, balloons came out!

Returning to town and the 'Big Croc', I sit with a group who are carving boab nuts again and talking. I even go on Peggy to get some more nuts for the fellas. I help a couple of people with eye issues and one with a painfully sprained ankle. The way this is turning out, it's much more of an informal assistance than my Army Brain imagined – just suggestions and advice, plus a little practical first aid. That's the way the people are comfortable with me helping. And to be honest, it just seems far more natural than any formal bush clinic. I am happy with the progress.

Today, I conducted a sport and recreation session with children. I'd hoped that will be a big hit, and as it happens, the sport and rec session could hardly have gone better. Loads of rowdy, excited children turn up and, in keeping with children this age, have this old, fat soldier on his toes. We do a little game called 'Stuck in the Mud' for an introduction, followed by some 'combat physical training' for a warm-up.

Then I introduce the kids to OZTAG, a great non-contact form of Rugby League. After a few hiccups, they get the idea and are very enthusiastic. I get to use my 40-year-old ACME thunderer whistle that creates a high-pitched blast, stopping or starting soldiers in their tracks. It was issued in 1982 on my selection to the APTC. The children are delightful in their enthusiasm, but quite a handful in their mischievousness. After the game, which is a tie, I am swamped with questions about soldiering, sharks and my trip around Australia.

Then, things go crazy as 20 kids all want to play with balloons and I can barely breathe as they swarm towards me, grasping and pulling at my clothes for their turn to have a balloon sword or animal made. It is such a great thing to have been given the opportunity to give joy to small kids, something I did with the YMCA for decades after leaving the UK. So, thank you to those involved for letting me bring a little activity session to your Sport and Recreation Area.

Before I started this mission, so many negative people said, "You will never do it," and "You will not be accepted," and "You are wasting your time and money." Well, they are all wrong! Human beings will always respond to love and respect. Children are innocent souls who just want some fun and love. Discrimination and hate should have no place in this world. If I had $10 for each negative comment I have received on Facebook and in discussions elsewhere, I could have paid for all my petrol to get here.

My intuition, communication skills and Peggy's charisma have made me a very happy, old soldier today.

DAY 22

Usual routine this morning – SSS (minus the shave), breakfast and change of stinky clothes, then into the bakery for a cup of coffee as I have run out. Meet some kids there again and I am accosted for balloons and even cake. I can't resist their smiles and big eyes so it's a coconut slice all round. Today is a 'work on Peggy' day, so up to 'the Croc' and get started.

There has to be a spanner in the works. 'Twas just that today. I am very much aware of keeping Peggy happy and doing routine maintenance in order to ensure we don't get stuck on some road in the top end. It has to be done – strip the luggage and get stuck in.

First step is to clean the chain and sprockets. The dust and sand up here, combined with chain lube, creates a very effective grinding paste. Out with the kerosene and paint brush to scrub the links and sprockets. This is a filthy job but without it, the drive and transmission could break. Once thoroughly scrubbed and soaked, I wash it off with water. Then comes the knuckle-stripping job on an Enfield – adjusting all the nuts and bolts placed where they're difficult to reach. I tend to shout a lot when a spanner slips, and I lose flesh. People look and wonder, *Who is that mad twat lying under that bike?* Anyone who has ever seen me cursing, swearing and getting spanner rash will tell you do not go near that raving lunatic.

Chain adjusted and cleaned – great. Now, onto the air cleaner, a very easy job really: remove, inspect and clean, replace. I then give Peggy a tub just to get rid of three weeks of outback dust, as well as crap from our 60 kilometre dirt trip to the Prison Tree.

After that, I'm invited to join a group at The Pond for lunch. The locals have just slaughtered a beast so it's fresh steaks cooked on the coals, with raw onion and bread. It's hot here today, so the campfire is purely for cooking.

Again, I'm asked for eye drops for very sore eyes that are exacerbated by rubbing and scratching. There really is no good reason why such things as trachoma should exist here in Australia; it is a constant source of frustration to me. It exists nowhere else in the developed world and is easily treated.

A little girl has an ankle and knee wound that I treated and dressed. Her knee isn't that bad, but the ankle wound's right on the joint and looks infected. I clean both up and dress the lesions, telling her to come tomorrow and I will change the dressing. I hope she does.

An extroverted local gentleman turns up in his beloved Toyota 4x4 in which he has installed a huge Chevy V8 engine. He's named the beast 'Big Daddy' and it sounds and goes like a tank on steroids. My friend, Joshua, is always telling me Toyotas are the vehicle of choice in these communities and after seeing so many, I am convinced he is right.

I leave the group shortly afterwards to get some food and coffee for the next couple of days and to type this sitrep (soldier speak for 'situation report') up for readers.

I have been invited to join the Elders again this evening. So, I walk up to The Pond later, leaving Peggy in base camp, and meet up with a bunch of kids and some local Elders. We light a fire and talk of the hard life in the region, such as their forced eviction from their ancestral home of Oombulgurri across the Cambridge gulf, and their horrific experiences of suicides in the town. Such resilient people! They have little and probably don't know how much the east coast and Australia has.

Next time you feel somewhat deprived, google 'Indigenous life in the Kimberley'.

I have already mentioned, the Kimberley is three times the size of England. If it were a country, it would have the dubious record of having the highest suicide rate in the world. That record is hardly a surprise when you are embedded with these strong people, who exist in conditions that provide little hope for the future and with the feeling that no one really cares for their plight. In fact, children as young as ten have taken their own lives here! The Elders tell me of two recent deaths where bodies of young men were found hanging from trees or shot in the head, as a result of loss of hope and opportunity.

They freely admit alcohol can be an issue. However, my thoughts drift to my own culture of motorcycle rallies, pubs with mates, and Army shenanigans. We are little different, and often drink to excess. As for smoking? Well, yes, most blackfellas smoke, but not 20 to 40 per day from tailor-made packs. They share a little roll up around groups, as they can't afford the decadent chain-smoking we see in our affluent towns and cities. If I were to estimate, I'd say five to ten roll ups were shared on any given day.

The conversation turns to where I have laid down my swag, right next to a dried-up creek in the small caravan park. When the creek has some water in it, there are often big saltwater crocodiles in its muddy waters. I've mentioned earlier an attack there, and now I'm given the details by an eyewitness. It happened a few years ago. An elderly lady with dementia walked down to the bank, saw the croc and decided to hand feed it like a dog. Well, unfortunately, the expected happened! It took her hand and arm and did a death roll, tearing off her arm at the elbow and ate it. The poor woman walked to the main road, calmly flagged down a car and asked to be taken to hospital holding the bleeding stump.

That is not the end of the story. The grandmother was more concerned about losing her wedding ring. The hunt was on, and the reptile was caught by throwing in a hooked fishing line which impaled it, and it was dragged out and summarily despatched and gutted. The half-digested arm was recovered with the wedding ring intact! Apparently, the little old dowager was very happy. The story is shocking, but I cannot help but find it somewhat amusing, and the Elders also have a chuckle. All's well that ends well.

DAY 23

I rise to the sound of a helicopter landing this morning at 0500. It's one of those little petrol engine jobs used here for mustering cattle. As a combat medic in the RAMC, I became very familiar with helicopters – part of the job. I have to say the jockeys who fly these little fragile toys within an inch of trees and ground deserve respect. An engine or rotor failure would most likely be catastrophic. An auto rotate to landing manoeuvre (a skill used by pilots to land a stricken helicopter using the energy stored in the rotating blades) almost certainly results in severe spinal injuries. Anyway, good on the courageous pilots – rather you than me.

It's time for SSS, breakfast, coffee, bakery then to cruise locally, meet groups, and watch Mr Bean carve some more boab nuts. He really is a character, loud, funny, obnoxious and engaging; a blackfella version of myself, I think.

After some time at The Pond in the heat of a Wyndham winter, I mount Peggy and return to the 'Big Croc' where my friend and former Norforce

(North-West Mobile Force) soldier is sitting. He takes great delight in telling me of his days in the Army as a private, such as the time he was dropped by parachute into the crocodile-infested waters off Darwin – no big deal to him. We are sitting and he is carving, when a tall, stately-looking gent with a walking stick, gingerly limps towards us. He states his name in a very clear English accent. Reginald Birch, OAM, no less.

Reginald is a musician and an artist, as well as having been a 'sportsman, rigger, diver, stock worker, tourist guide, fisherman, community worker and political activist'. He was born at the Forrest River Mission and spent time living around the Wyndham and Kimberley areas. He has represented the Indigenous community at local, state, national and international levels. While living in Canberra, he worked at the Council for Aboriginal Development and the Aboriginal and Torres Strait Islander Commission (ATSIC).

In 1977, Birch was selected to represent the Kimberley at the National Aboriginal Conference, a role he held until 1981. This position gave him the opportunity to be the South Pacific representative to the World Council of Indigenous People. From 1982 to 1985, he chaired the State Advisory Committee for the Aboriginal Lands Trust. He had the opportunity to be the ATSIC Commissioner of Northern Western Australia twice. Birch helped form the Kimberley Land

Council (KLC) and chaired the council from 1988 to 1990.

One of Birch's personal highlights in his life was when he co-supervised the process of returning Aboriginal remains from universities and other institutions overseas. This man has wined and dined with the powerful and rich, even meeting the Queen on two occasions. He has been a representative for the world's Indigenous people at the United Nations. He invited me back to his historic home with its fence made up of all and sundry: ploughs, cartwheels, truck parts, dingo traps, and so on.

What a character! His mother was part of the Stolen Generations, deemed a 'half-caste' and his father was a hard Scotsman with a wooden leg. I could have listened to his stories for hours. He told me of catching crocs with his bare hands. As a boy in the '40s and '50s, he had to collect the human faecal waste and dead bodies from the local leper colony. He nearly lost his foot when a train at the meat works ran over his ankle in the 1960s and he had to run on the broken, bleeding stump for many yards to get help. He rescued a young mother and baby who fell off the jetty into the crimson waters of the crocodile-infested water of the 'blood drain' near the abattoir and was chased by said reptiles many times.

He tells me of his people being chained and hunted down with rifles, like dogs, whilst digging and clearing the stock routes above Wyndham on the Bastion Ridge; killed or left to die in the blazing sun as late as in the 1950s. He shows me his paintings depicting these events and many more. His graphic art is stupendous and testament to his memory and the enduring horror of what he has witnessed.

He knows many of the First Nations people in 'high political office', having worked with them over many years. He has little good to say about them, only that they have let his people down, reminding me of George Orwell's pigs in *Animal Farm* rewriting the rules of equality: 'four legs good, two legs better'. He lives out his life as an outcast, as he has rocked their boat too many times and made himself a target, choosing to be a thorn in the system's side; an 'activist', he calls himself. He is a staunch advocate for Indigenous people worldwide. Meeting Reg, seeing his drawings and listening to his experiences, has a profound effect on me. It both makes me angry and more determined to tell this story. I am extremely impressed by this great man, his tenacity, and his devotion to his people.

Later in the day, Peggy and I go back to the school's recreation centre to entertain children again. I am hoping to run games and relay races but it's Friday here and most kids are either at home or doing other stuff, so there's not enough numbers. Never mind – 'Mr Balloon' remains popular, and the children love it, so balloons it is. We spend about 40 minutes with the kids being a goose, something that seems to come easily to this old Corpsman.

Tonight, being my penultimate night here, I go to the pond gathering place where people assemble. I sit with my friends. Mr Bean is here, being his entertaining self. Much to my surprise, I am initiated to the region by the Elders. Suddenly, Mr Bean and another Elder light a branch of gum leaves and ask me to stand. I can see the flames and embers glowing in the dark of a Kimberley night as they approach me and say, "This is to bring you in and will give you the protection of our people and serpent." They then gently start beating my body and legs.

I am apprehensive, as the last thing I need are burns. I need not have been concerned. I am enveloped in the smoke, smelling burning gum and being told to breathe in the smoke. Thus, they give me an honour, the smoking ceremony. I am taken aback, but they tell me the Indigenous people of the Kimberley would smell me and know I am admitted and protected.

This is not some trite little thing they did. These ancient people have a history of at least 60,000 years. Whilst they worship no gods here, the people are very spiritual and believe in The Dreaming, telling me of the Dark Emu in the Milky Way and the giant serpent living in their waterways.

They also tell me more about their old community, Oombulgurri, their traditional lands not far away from which they had been forcibly removed during the 'Intervention' of that 'war criminal' John Howard's making ten years ago. They were forced to live in the township of Wyndham, severing their connection with homelands.

An all too familiar story for the Indigenous people of the world when whitefellas take over. It starts with the removal of services like clinics, a shop here and there, and what little electricity there is cut off. Then, when the stalwart people refuse to leave, they are removed by force, and their structures are bulldozed, much like their history has been.

Sometimes, I despair at the cruelty and methods our culture uses to destroy theirs – 60,000 years destroyed in less than 200. I'm given two photos of the avenue of boab trees through their home Oombe. It looks lush and green and inviting.

Now gone, lost, like the homes that were buried by the state.

Back at base, I type this up and post yet another day in the Kimberley. The Kimberley Races tomorrow may prove fun on the dustbowl track. I hope no one needs my help.

DAY 24

Today starts very cool for a change. I've got to take advantage of that in my morning routine. It's Wyndham Race Day and I've never seen a horse race in the desert, so I'm keen to go. I get all prepared in my best bib and tucker. Peggy and I drive up only about a kilometre from town to the track, not knowing what to expect.

First thing that strikes me is the sea of white-fellas; not one local is in sight. People are 'dressed to the nines' with fascinators on heads, and in suits and ties. I'm wearing an Indigenous design shirt and made to feel quite unwelcome in my attire. Questioned three times about my dress, I become a little anxious. I am not exaggerating when I say I feel like I am in South Africa in the 1970s. Security is swanning around, and I know when I am under watch; situational awareness is something all good soldiers become familiar with.

Still, despite the obvious, I remain, as I really want a photo of a horse race in the sand of the far north. Once I've achieved this lofty goal, I cannot wait to leave – no way am I staying with people who make me feel this way.

I return to Wyndham and The Pond. The black-fellas gathered there apologise to me for not warning me about the reception I may get in the garb I'm wearing. They also point out my presence has been noticed. The fact I have been spending time with blackfella groups may not go down well with some local influential whitefellas. Ah, well, ho hum. It's the whitefellas' loss. I am the life and soul at parties. No 'balloon models' for those that follow equestrian pursuits. I'm back with the folk who have accepted me as a friend.

It's my last night in Wyndham for a while and I sit with the community talking by a fire as the night quickly falls, and we are under the Milky Way yet again. Most people slowly drift away from the camp by the pond, leaving just one Elder and me warming ourselves in the amber glow and having a couple of beers.

Suddenly, a car approaches at speed across the dusty ground, headlights on full beam and a huge light bar blazing and dazzling us both. It pulls up sharply about a metre away. I think it's 'Big Daddy' in his hot Toyota.

I am wrong. It's the cops.

Immediately they start intimidating my companion – funny how they just give me a filthy look. They chastise him in a very aggressive manner for drinking. If they had spoken to me like that,

I would have chewed their face off. We two old men just sit there as the young, 30-something who probably has been nowhere, seen nothing, says (whilst waving his finger), "No mischief and you two behave yourselves!" My friend is obviously a little scared and becomes quiet, agreeing with the officer. At that point, the divvy wagon backs up, spraying dust around, and takes off faster than he arrived. Classic example of the separatist nature of policing and law in the far north of WA.

After that, we say goodnight and I go back to my swag.

Tomorrow I'm on to a far more remote spot in the Kimberley called Turkey Creek and Doon Doon. I have networks there now, thanks to Wyndham folk. I don't know if I will have the benefit of an internet repeater station to update my blog, but I will try.

DAY 25

In the morning, striking my ten-day old camp is preceded by the usual SSS. Then, I pack Peggy, the two wheeled mule, and head to the bakery for one last Wyndham coffee. First stop, a hundred kilometres into Kununurra to restock eye drops and Panadol. Then, it is back to the Great Northern Highway turnoff to Halls Creek and our destination of Warmun (Turkey Creek).

This road goes right through the centre of the Kimberley, snaking through some of the most spectacular geological landscapes. The oldest rocks on Earth, burnt and eroded. On one side of the road, vertical red sedimentary cliffs rise steeply from the rock-strewn terrain. On the other side, enormous granite slabs, tors and slopes dominate the visa. Both are entirely different in their origins, but just held apart by a thin strip of broken tarmac.

Peggy is happy – she overtakes her first road train today. It takes a while, but she does it, only to be passed again on a flat section of this remote highway. This is something I never become accustomed to – just looking straight ahead ignoring the leviathan only inches away and hoping the driver knows how long his truck actually is. Once safe, I flash my lights and wave to let him pull back in.

First fuel stop is Doon Doon, where I meet a small family and Mr Balloon comes out to play. Turns out the family knows Mr Bean in Wyndham. These people are all family, all brothers, sisters, aunties and uncles, even if there is no genetic connection. The land connects them all, despite being hundreds of kilometres apart. They are genuinely connected and know what is going on in the region.

Now I have arrived safely in Warmun – a dry community. No grog on sale here! I will try to embed here for a week or so getting to know the community, doing some first aid and hopefully games for the kids. Balloons are already a hit.

I'm setting up my swag in the back of the Warmun Roadhouse, immediately getting settled. It's hardly a pleasant spot, with mud, mozzies and so on, but at least there is a dunny can and a grotty shower. Times like these, Army training allows you to accept less than hygienic conditions.

They have a little cafe here, so I can get a bacon buttie and coffee tomorrow. There are loads of children here, arriving in cars packed to the gunnels, and piling out enthusiastically. Peggy is flavour of the month and Mr Balloon has a lot of business keeping all the little ones happy. The roadhouse closes at 2000 hours and families from Warmun Community stop coming. So, it's time for my sleeping bag (green maggot) under my mosquito net.

DAY 26

I again wake to the early morning chorus of Aussie songbirds and crows. There's no point in lying there at 0500, so I'm up and get my little stove going, making the first shot of caffeine today. Then, I get all scrubbed up and ready to introduce myself to the locals.

I walk around to the roadhouse. Before I get close, I am approached by a man in a grey t-shirt and shorts, Aussie style (or no style, really). I am in trouble again – nothing new for me! The children had disposed of their balloons in the manner of all kids worldwide – on the ground! I get that, and he asks me not to entertain children at the roadhouse, and I get that also. I am very apologetic and promise not to do it again. All good until his final comment as he stares me down, "I know you are trying to do cute things for 'EM! But THEY don't respect it and will just drop it out their ARSE when done."

They are just kids being kids and I support his rights to a tidy workplace, but he's given his true discriminatory game away. This community is his living; without it, there would be no roadhouse and he should demonstrate more respect.

Onwards and upwards, to find a niche here in their hearts and minds. I visit the local arts centre, a small place displaying the art of local Indigenous people. I wish I could take photos because the works are completely in tune with the landscape, using mainly ochres from the region. But googling Warmun Arts Centre finds the images. I also meet two of the local puppies here, very friendly, but a local blackfella has warned me – the dogs here are a big risk and may attack strangers without warning. So, I approach with caution.

Whilst in there, I bump into the local ambulance officer and he says, "We could have used you last night." Apparently, a man in his car hit a Brahman bull at 110 kilometres an hour. He suggests I go look. Well, the end of the story is, the driver survived with a broken arm and minor cuts and grazes. He needs to buy a lottery ticket ASAP. I have seen many cars cut to pieces by the Jaws of Life in my career as a Firefighter, but this damage is entirely due to the massive impact. The bull, whilst swollen by the heat, is still at least one and a half tons and the biggest I have seen to date. Those are some of the risks when driving these arid remote roads. I think I'd rather deal with 70 metre road trains.

Peggy and I go to the local school and meet with the principal to arrange fun, games, storytelling, and balloons for the children of this very tight, dry community. We have also been contacted by Fairfax Media. They are coming 200 kilometres to Warmun to do a 'face to face' piece. As far as I'm concerned, any publicity that highlights the issues in the Kimberley is a great thing; that's turning out to be the thrust of Peggy and my mission.

As I sit at the roadhouse, a small convoy of Army trucks pulls in and a group of Indigenous soldiers and their Sergeant Major dismount for morning tea. We start a conversation, and I find they are passing this way going to South Broome. They are interested and very keen to get a picture with Peggy. Who am I to stop Peggy making more male friends?

Because Warmun is a dry community, not much goes on after dark in terms of the roadhouse. It pretty much closes at about 8.00pm, so I spend my time writing up my blog and reading the book, *Wyndham Yella Fella*, by Reginald Birch, OAM. It is a great read about the arduous life of a black-fella growing up in the Kimberleys. Some of his anecdotes are shocking, some amusing, but all is an education in a life well lived, despite overwhelming odds. I thoroughly recommend it to anyone inter-ested in the reality of Kimberley life. One part to note is where Reg has to go with his father to col-lect the dead bodies of lepers who have passed away from this dreadful disease. Hansen's Disease is not gone here. To this day, people in the Kimberley suffer its ravages.

Just getting started here – let's see what comes of my first contacts in Warmun. A good night's sleep, only broken by someone moving around in a suspicious manner. My hypervigilance born of my training alerts me and with a quick shout they disappear into the night.

DAY 27

Today is about more networking, so Peggy and I ride into Warmun to meet the friend of Mr Bean in Wyndham. I go to his place and introduce myself. He is a big, strong-looking fella, and he greets me with a firm handshake. We sit down in the shade at the rear of his home surrounded by four or five friendly dogs. We speak of Mr Bean and his association, and also of the difficulty I may have when accessing this closed community. He gives me some tips and names of people and places I should visit. He recommends I go to the Community Centre and speak with them about any recreation activities we may help with.

So, with that, Peggy and I ride over to the Offices. There, we meet the CEO of this closed community, where access by the outside world is heavily restricted by sanction of locals and whitefellas. She appears to be a whitefella administrator appointed and paid by the WA government to manage and protect the local people. We are there to get permission to enter and interact, as communities like this restrict any negative influence of outside influences, alcohol or passers-by.

I have a good talk with her and fill out the obligatory forms, present my Working with Children check, first aid certificates and so forth. Only then, do I get permission to enter.

Unfortunately for me, the children are away on a camp with the recreation officer, so no games or balloon animals until they return on Friday. Warmun is a well-resourced community, and its people are happy, friendly and enjoy meeting us at the roadhouse, perhaps because they are left to manage their own affairs in the main.

Peggy and I take off south down the road, looking for photo ops. We meet a stalwart Frenchman who has been walking hundreds of kilometres through the Kimberleys towing a mono wheeled hand cart. Quite an undertaking in this heat! Wrapped in protective garb, he tells me he is feeling very unwell and thought he may have been bitten. The mozzies up here carry all manner of viruses. I ask if he needs help or water. He is reluctant to accept assistance and says he will keep going the seven kilometres to Warmun. I tell him I will be at the caravan park if he changes his mind.

We also meet with a handsome but tired looking young man in dirty, grey motorcycle clothing. He is from Sydney and is touring the north of Australia. He is going to ride his BMW motorcycle over to the Bungle Bungles, a strange iconic rock formation not that far away, and then take on the infamous and tough Gibb River Road. Good on him for LIVING LIFE LARGE!

I have a restless night, excited from meeting again with the Frenchman, who arrives at the Warmun Roadhouse where we exchanged pleasantries and information. He is an adventurer walking across the Kimberley with his home and survival gear in his single wheeled cart. This undertaking is extraordinary, when you consider he has done over 1700 kilometres on foot through the wilderness and visited remote communities on the way. Turns out, he is also a huge advocate for First Nations rights and the Yellow Shirts of Paris. He is walking the Kimberley to support and raise awareness of crimes against Australian Aboriginal culture. He, like me, has been saddened and challenged by the conditions, poor health and disadvantages he has seen. He is well-read and understands the issues extremely well.

He is also very interested in Peggy and the *Muriel the Medicycle* program. He wants to know the military history behind Peggy Pegasus (The Flying Flea), so I explain the story of Operation Market Garden in 1944, in which the parachute regiment was tasked with taking and holding a bridge in Arnhem, famously told in the movie, *A Bridge Too Far.* Having heard Peggy's story, he tells me he is from the Arnhem region and regularly rows his boat under that very bridge. Now,

I don't know what other people think, but I call that synchronicity of the highest order: Two people connected by a mission and then by WW2 history? This is meant to happen! We speak late into the Western Australian night.

I retire with a very active mind, some of which happened due to the aggressive roadhouse manager who cannot get over the kids enjoying balloons and stories. He has asked me to stop talking with locals, insisting I sit in the caravan park. I think one more night here and we will move on to another area and see if we can entertain or help there.

Tomorrow, we have an appointment with Fairfax Media. They are interested in Peggy's story. Then, I'm on to bigger and better things further into the Kimberley region.

DAY 28

I give my spot and two days stay at the park to the Frenchman and leave for pastures new, riding north again, to Doon Doon community about a hundred kilometres away. The road snakes through the same magical russet canyons I rode four days ago, but the sun has a different perspective, and the light creates enigmatic shadows and colours on the landscape and big boab trees.

When I arrive at the Doon Doon Roadhouse I am greeted by a lovely Indigenous woman, who is an Elder, and has said she will take Peggy and me into the community, introducing us to the school and its children. Before that, however, are subjects of the gastronomic kind, as I left Warmun without breakfast, not wanting to meet with the cranky manager again. I eat the most appetizing cheeseburger just the way I like it: meat patty, melted cheese, raw red onion and tomato sauce... perfect!

Waiting with Peggy is like waiting with a celebrity – everyone wants to know her story, which I am happy to regurgitate a thousand times, finishing off with, "Watch the movie."

As promised, I am taken into the tiny remote community of Doon Doon. We venture to the Elder's home and meet her children and her partner, a proud, handsome-looking man with a friendly attitude and smile. It's funny, though – the eldest of the three girls must have sensed from Peggy's red cross that I'm a travelling medic, because she immediately starts showing me the wound on her foot. So cute.

Next, we visit the little school with six students and I meet the principal, a happy, engaging young woman with a welcoming handshake and smile a mile wide. Lovely! I explain what I am doing and all about Peggy, and we arrange for me to entertain the children. I am coming back tomorrow with my documentation, including my 'Working with Children' Check and 'Working with Vulnerable People Check' and to complete some forms. I get shown around the tiny school in the 40 degree heat of the day. School starts at 0600 to avoid most of the heat.

We leave for the kind Elder's home again and I offer to clean up the wound on her daughter's foot and dress it. As it is a little infected, I pay attention to cleaning it, and a good dressing is applied, covered up by the cut off wrist section of a rubber glove to keep it clean. I give them more dressings, antiseptic and band aids. This little community has a clinic, but it is only open once a month. For any

pressing matters, people need to travel 180 kilometres to Kununurra. This beautiful family are
travelling to Wyndham tomorrow for a funeral,
such is the connected nature of Indigenous people
in the Kimberley.

After a lovely time with them and visiting the
tiny, remote but very loved little school and its principal, we arrange to talk again tomorrow and maybe
some balloon modelling with the children.

I return to the well-appointed and very new
campsite to erect a camp for the night.

With time on my hands, I want to see some local
attractions, hills and rivers that contain the mighty
barramundi, making this spot popular with fisher-
men. I ride north to a large bridge crossing the river
at the base of some impressive red crags. The river
is a fair way down and its level is very low due to
the extended drought and lack of a real wet season
for a few years. With this in mind, and knowing
the crocs are more dangerous hiding in the pools,
I just take some photos and leave for camp back at
Doon Doon.

Preparing dinner and drinks is good here, with
great BBQ facilities and tables making it easy. The
light fades and it's soon time for sleep, as it is always
early to rise here.

Wow, what a night! Doon Doon is situated in a
flat valley, with mountainous craggy ranges rising
either side. The movement of air as the day heats or
cools is dramatic. As I lie under my mosquito net

on my sleep mat, the winds are howling in different directions. At times, I feel the speed of a willy willy flying around like the Looney Tunes character, Tassie Devil.

DAY 29

Despite the windy conditions, I get a good night's sleep, only waking as the sun peeps over the range to my east. The roadhouse here is a good one, despite the remoteness, and serves good food. As the manager points out, it's a new area for the Grey Nomads to park their RVs and caravan rigs. I take advantage of the clean facilities and have a shower and clean up. Breakfast is a little different. They served a very nice savoury mince on toast. 'Being a little peckish-like' (a saying from the famous Monty Python cheese shop sketch), I avail myself, and top up on coffee.

Going over to the school as arranged, I am welcomed by the principal. We discuss entertaining the children with balloons and stories etc. After checking my documentation, it's been found that my Working with Children and Working with Vulnerable People certification is not valid over here in Western Australia. Such is life; the world is a different place these days, so I accept that in good faith.

As there is a big funeral in the region today and many blackfellas are travelling to Wyndham, not a lot is happening. While I am here writing my blog, a chap from Warmun, who is on his way to the funeral, stops briefly for a chat. He is very kind and chats happily, telling me the children in Warmun were disappointed I'd left the roadhouse and expressed their dislike of the manager's decision about the balloons. I think that's lovely of him to let me know this, and it lifts my spirits again. He tells me of his service in the Australian Army (Norforce) and how much he loves Peggy, so I offer him the opportunity for a photo with Peggy. He is so enthusiastic and genuine that I am thankful for his company.

I have been advised to beware of my personal safety in the Kimberleys, but so far, the only people I have met who make me anxious and tense are my own generation of whitefellas. So, with that in mind, I head off on the 250 kilometres to Halls Creek.

This part of my plans has brought me anxiety since I decided a year ago to return. The community there is predictably angry with whitefellas; you can cut the atmosphere with a knife. The people are suffering more than most from discrimination, disenfranchisement, disease and deprivation, but the town is central in the Kimberley at the junction of Highway One and other remote roads. It has more than its fair share of touring baby boomers travelling in luxury, whilst the locals' conditions are dire. Last year, when visiting, I noted the caravan park has high security fences, guards and dogs patrolling. People swan through, leaving little to improve the lives of First Nations people here. I am not surprised at the sense of disdain the blackfellas emanate.

DAY 30

On the way to Halls Creek, the heart of the Kimberley, the dead centre, is massive cattle station country. Stations are marked and they go on for hundreds of kilometres. Each one would exceed millions of acres, with millions of cattle roaming the region. The road is bordered with dry rough ground, a few cabbage gums and massive red termite mounds looking like Jabba the Hutt, spying at you as you ride on.

Arriving in Halls Creek, the first feeling I get is that I am in a frontier town. It reminds me of an old western: it's hot and dry like the surrounding landscape. The main street looks like something from the '70s in post-war Glasgow – old derelict run-down houses and shops abound, and litter is everywhere. It does not have a welcoming feel. This is a town of contrasts, much like Elliott, Utopia and Wyndham. It is unofficially segregated, with the whitefellas in their opulent RVs and caravans, and the Indigenous folk who sit or wander around, many looking very poor, sick or deprived. Last time

I was here, it was much busier with tourists, but they leave little here for the blackfellas. All the businesses are owned by whitefellas.

My plan is to do some shopping for my camp this evening. I am opting for a bush camp somewhere in the scrub. It's lazy here today but still I get a bad vibe in this place.

I am approached by a local lady. She was curious about Peggy. When we get talking, I find out that she is a health worker here. She loves the idea of my mission, saying she wishes there were more initiatives such as *Muriel the Medicycle*.

"There should be more of it," she said. "There is such a need. The local blackfellas call it Hell's Crack."

I'm happy. She's made me feel better as I'm anxious being here, and especially so getting the visual once-over from the cops in their divvy van.

A lady in the street approaches me for food. I'm probably suckered, but I buy her some corned beef to cook. It's extremely expensive. It would have cost $8.00 in Bombala, but here it's $26.00. FFS!

I meet another guy, an interesting character much like Mr Bean. He actually knows Reginald Birch in Wyndham and tells me I just got ripped off. I laugh, hey ho! He tells me how his country has been stolen from his people and we have turned his people into dependent bludgers. A dignified man, he hates how his proud race has been usurped by colonial forces.

This place truly is an apartheid town – anyone can see that! Anyway, I am angry and want to continue talking with him, an interesting Elder with strong opinions concerning his people, his town and its future. He laments the loss of his people's culture, much like Reginald Birch in Wyndham does. He is scathing in his opinions about the effects of much of whitefella culture, such as handouts, football and excess alcohol, but he remains very cognisant of the crimes blackfellas have suffered over many decades. He willingly tells me of beatings, killings and deaths in custody he has witnessed over his long life.

He is more than aware of the health issues facing blackfellas in this place. He tells me of introduced diseases such as syphilis and other STDs that are ravaging this community. He says some women sell sex for money to buy alcohol which only serves to spread these conditions. He is a very intelligent man and says much on the historical and present neglect and manipulation of his folk. He is very amusing in his narrative, witnessing over 60 years in the Kimberley, and has me laughing out loud many times. His scathing opinions of "so-called Indigenous art" and the obsession with football are very enlightening and funny.

Speaking of alcohol, I'm gagging for a beer, so I ride to the bottle shop to partake. There, I meet another interesting Indigenous man, whose European family line goes back to 1629 when his ancestors, two young boys, were marooned by the Captain of a Dutch ship called *The Batavia* in order to save rations. This happened north of Gerald-ton WA. Fortunately, his Dutch ancestors found fresh water, and further inland met local people, the Nanda, who took them on, becoming the seed of many mixed generations. He says his DNA was traced back to the family of those same boys in Hol-land, centuries later in a land claim by his people. This is a refreshing and informative interlude with a blackfella who's employed here. I say, 'thank you' and 'goodbye' to him and mount my steed, Peggy, to find a campsite in the bush.

One of the first things you notice about Halls Creek is it's a town under siege. Every establish-ment has high fences barbed, and sometimes with razor wire surrounding. When I'd asked about this I was told, "Gangs patrol the town and will break in anywhere, given the chance." My new friend was clearly saddened by the loss of hope in many young people and the world's highest suicide rate.

I am grateful to find a bush camp well out of Halls Creek. Taking advice, I keep lights out and noise to a minimum, simply a sensible precaution in this angry town. Once the mosquito net and camp are set, I cook dinner, have coffee and a Kit Kat for a treat. Like we used to say in the Army of the 1970s, "Any fool can be uncomfortable in the field."

As darkness falls, it's a fully-clothed-and-boots-on retirement to my swag. The skies are so

Bozo in a Beret

Graves of the
Afghan Cameleers,
buried with their
lead camels.

Utrinque paratus. Peggy
ready for anything.

Warriu Park
Dreamtime Statues
depicting an
Indigenous family.

Carving the Boab nut is a skill that is simply amazing to watch.

The Boab Prison Tree found just south of Wyndham, also known as the Hillgrove Lockup.

Fun and games with the local school kids in Wyndham.

Never drive at dusk or dawn in the Top End.

Another home for the night in the bush outside Halls Creek – trying to avoid the prying eyes of the police.

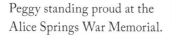

Peggy standing proud at the Alice Springs War Memorial.

clear the Milky Way stands out like nowhere else on the planet. The Dark Emu running across the skies signifies to Aboriginals that dry weather is to come. Eventually, I fall into oblivion and dream. That's short lived. Despite 40-plus temperatures during the day, the mercury plummets to near zero. I'm freezing and restless. I look up through the fine mesh and clearly see the large and small Magellanic galaxies to the south and Orion's Belt straight above me.

DAY 31

I toss and turn, but dawn eventually breaks at 0530, and it's time to get underway. Two coffees, beef, beans (and yet another Kit Kat), then I strike camp. Heading off for Halls Creek some kilometres away, I'm happy that I'd found such a secluded camp in the dry scrub.

As I sit in the centre of town waiting for everyone else to rise, I see my dignified, opinionated, and informative friend from yesterday. I'm taking a photo of the White Obelisk used as a cenotaph, and we strike up a conversation. He tells me of the origins of the large white sphere at the top of the structure, "That is the large iron ball to which my people were chained in the late 1800s and first half of the 1900s."

What does that say about the treatment of Aboriginals who fought for Australia in both world wars?

It strikes me dumb!

Close to it is a statue of *Russian Jack*, a gold miner of the 1860s who pushed his injured friend

300 kilometres in a makeshift barrow to find medical help. It may be my imagination, but the police divvy wagon is circling, and the police seem to have us under surveillance, as do the obvious moving security cameras placed everywhere around town.

Bored with town now, I take a ride out to the Old Halls Creek site which was the old telegraph office until the 1950s. In an arid, desolate place some 16 kilometres down a very corrugated road train route, the telegraph office is made of crushed termite mounds mixed with spinifex grass and water, a very ingenious and effective building material. The road is very difficult terrain, due in part to the dust on top of the corrugations. Peggy and I find it challenging. On the way, there is a memorial to all the helicopter pilots who've died in crashes mustering cattle in the Kimberley. That occupation looks as dangerous as the Isle of Man TT (Tourist Trophy), with so many recently lost. RIP, brave fellows.

Halls Creek seems to be lost to many here. So many people wander and sit around, obviously very sick mentally and physically, with little hope of improvement. It's hard to imagine how the children here will ever break the chains that have shackled their parents, grandparents, and ancestors. They seem destined to see repeating discrimination, disenfranchisement, deprivation, and disease. Surely, governments can find a solution for the blackfellas of the Kimberley! Band aids, bandages and balloons from Peggy and me only scratch the surface, but at least the locals know someone cares enough to shed light on the neglect here.

To think the Australian government recently gave $370,000,000 to Indonesia in official development assistance seems a little unjust to me, when our own children suffer in abject poverty.

DAY 32

I wake this morning to find my own Black Dog is biting. I find the sense that most blackfellas here have lost hope and speaking to them depresses my own psyche, and I have fought with the dark hound for years. I need to leave this place in the centre of the Kimberleys. One month on the road and two weeks in this region is stretching me. The fact this frontier town has such a high suicide rate is not lost on me.

Anyway, I have work to do today. Peggy needs a proper service ensuring her faithful, thumping heart keeps going for at least another six weeks in the remote outback. She's a simple beast but beware the big spring that can fire the oil filter housing into the dirt, along with the small retaining bolts. Fortunately, I felt the pressure and my mind said, *Hold it, slowly does it*. So, all's good. My mate, Joshua, is an expert on Royal Enfield and would understand. This (and numerous other checks) takes a while, but is thankfully done early before the heat kicks in.

The main form of recreation here seems to be

hanging around the servo, much to the dislike of its owner and the Grey Nomads filling their fuel tanks. I really stink and I need a shower, but that will have to wait. The lady who runs the caravan park here says she can no longer let 'drop-ins' shower. I met her last year. We have a short chat about the increasing problems of theft and violence in the town and the effects they are having on the travellers passing through. She comes across as a lovely person and has a beaming pearly white smile. I can't resist talking for longer.

Next on the agenda today is to check Peggy's tyre pressures and then get some rations for tonight, which may include chocolate and tinnies of light beer, as that's all that is available here. At the moment, I am in the only pub, rehydrating – in the best sense of the word! When done, I will head back out on the Great Northern Highway towards my campsite. Then, after some sleep, it's back on the road and another stop over at Wyndham.

For my return journey, I'm thinking of the long run down the Stuart Highway to Port Augusta, stopping at small communities, as I see fit. I'm looking at another month of that. I'm really missing my loving whippet puppy, Loretta. Thankfully, my good friend, Anthony, is still taking care of her and sending photos of her pushing him out of his bed.

Tonight is my last night in Hell's Crack, because I find Halls Creek a very challenging place to stay, albeit for only three nights. I feel unsafe; I feel the depressive aura that exists there and speaking with blackfella mates only confirms my own thoughts.

Back at the town store and just when I am at a very low ebb, I'm accosted by several children. Word has got round Mr Balloon is in town. I've only gone to buy some chilli stew for tea at my bush camp when I'm set upon. It's fun; it's lifted my spirits, even though they are little rascals and full of mischief. We block the door to the shop doing balloon models, but people passing by are smiling.

One young lady, a teacher, finally gets hold of her prodigal student and asks, "Where have you been?" The little scallywag has been wagging school. He doesn't seem to care one little bit, he's more occupied with a balloon sword fight with his mates.

Happy interlude over, Peggy and I ride out of Halls Creek to our bush camp for the last time. Darkness falls quickly in the north-west, at about 1730; no daylight saving here. As the sun sets, the temperature drops nearly as quickly, and a cool breeze sets in.

I cook the tin of chilli and, after dinner, do some work and make phone calls. I try to stay as close to each transmitter as I can. That way, I can update and stay in touch because there's mostly no signal out here.

DAY 33

At the break of dawn, sun just peeking over the dark red horizon, my son Harrison rings to wish me a happy Father's Day, a nice surprise as I'd forgotten. I have a quick coffee then strike camp, do an 'emu bob' then get the 'feek' out of here.

On to the Great Northern Highway. One never gets sick of this wilderness scenery, and we get a special treat today. Up ahead, I see a large cloud of spiralling orange dust. I'm thinking it's a dust storm until I see a tiny toy helicopter mustering a herd of cattle. They excitedly run exactly where the rotor wash pushes them. The pilot has the whole mob completely under control as it dances amongst the trees and plays 'fiddle with the devil'.

When I reach my turn back to Wyndham, it's getting dry and hot. I'd heard about this place called the Grotto, a little waterfall and pond at the base of some sheer sandstone cliffs. Peggy and I just have to have a look at such a cooling place in the arid rocky landscape of the Kimberley. I walk in and climb down some broken rock steps. There are some young people there, cooling off in the water and doing impressive back flips off the large branch of a tree anchored halfway up the cliff. Apparently, the water depth here is over a hundred metres. That's much deeper than normal scuba divers can go; one can only imagine the dark depths at the bottom. Of course, there are crocodiles, I hear you ask. But only the relatively harmless freshwater species. Having said that, a lady was bitten recently. I have to have a swim to cool off.

The kids say, "It's bloody cold!"

I reply, "Mate! You have never been cold. I am from Yorkshire."

It's lovely in, swimming around for half an hour or so, talking with the 'young uns'! I make a white balloon swan for them, and it floats quite well. They think it's cool. I tell them it will biodegrade very quickly but take it with them anyway.

Soon, I am in Wyndham again for Rest & Recuperation before the next part of this long journey. I go to wash my clothes and have a shower at the pleasant little caravan park here. Some kids come in, trying to sell me some Aboriginal art and get short-shifted out by staff. Funnily though, some of the Elders I've met say the contemporary style of dot painting is not true historical Indigenous art. They said they do not know its origins, but it has now become synonymous in Western culture so that's what sells. Apparently, dot painting has its origins 40 years ago, in 1971. A gent called

Geoffrey Bardon was assigned as an art teacher for the children of the Aboriginal people in Papunya, near Alice Springs. He noticed the Elders telling stories by making marks and dots in the sand, and helped develop the art form we now see as Australian Indigenous art. So, it would appear my opinionated elderly friend from Halls Creek had a point!

This morning, regardless, brings the luxury of a shower and clean clothes after a week on the road through Central Kimberley. Soon after, I go to the pie shop and have a locally caught barramundi pie with garlic for breakfast. It's delicious!

Despite resting from the journey, I just have to pay a longer visit to Reginald Birch OAM, so Peggy and I ride to his home. He greets us in his eclectic front yard, and we sit in the shade and rapidly rising temps, discussing his book and life in the Kimberley. I'm curious to ask why he feels this region and its Indigenous people seem to be left behind by mainstream Australia. He suggests the tyranny of distance, lack of political will and a system that wants to control this land and its people for the rich resources, minerals and gas lying underground have all led to the traditional ways, and owners, dying out. He has fought the system for 50 years and says it will take two or more generations for Indigenous folk to be assimilated into whitefella paradigms. He laments this but is cognisant he will not be around much longer.

I don't want to get too serious at the moment. I am tired, so I go to The Pond with a six pack to share with a few people. Jeez, it's hot today! So, what better way to 'wet your whistle' than with a tinnie or two? The irrepressible Mr Bean is there, so for our amusement we make a short video discussing what he does each day. People who can make you laugh and share joy are rare these days. He has charisma and I like him.

Two other characters are there. My original soldier mate and his friend, who is a really nice older guy like me, with a very kind, caring persona. The former soldier with Norforce loves to pull up a sandbag and tell warrior stories about his youth as a soldier and paratrooper jumping from aircraft. His friends just smile. I can tell they don't believe him, but his explanations tell me he is speaking the truth.

Not much else is on as I rest up before extending Peggy even further right through Australia's massive dry heart.

DAY 34

It's said: *'A picture paints a thousand words'*. I think about the illustrations drawn by Wyndham Elder and Statesman, Reginald Birch (Order of Australia Medal), depicting life for many blackfellas in the Kimberley, all within living memory. Lest we forget crimes committed by colonists and others.

A few that spring to mind include the image of his mother being forcefully kidnapped by police as a child. The trauma in this drawing was apparent and touched me deeply.

Another shows the picture of a dying slave who could not keep up on the chain gang. His neck chain was removed, and he was left to die in the sun, with crows and kite hawks pecking at his eyes and flesh.

Finally, the artwork featuring yet another chain gang digging stock routes over the high ground in 50 degree heat. A police officer with a Winchester rifle stands guard ready to shoot any escapees, who are all dressed in white to make them easier targets.

WE ALL NEED TO KNOW ABOUT THESE ATROCITIES!

I spend a good deal of time with Reg today. I really need to understand what I am witnessing.

DAY 35

After nearly three weeks crossing and camping in the Kimberley, Peggy and I are actually moving closer to home now – and my puppies. We've a long way to go yet, though. Probably six weeks more with Peggy and more swag camping. However, the emotional lift I am getting is huge!

So, a wrap up of our nearly three weeks in the Kimberley (actually a month if you count our circumnavigation last year).

Much of this time we enjoyed the company of Indigenous people of the region. We learned much about their true history and what life is like for these proud people. The Aboriginal people of the Kimberley have long memories and a strong oral history which is passed down; they are all connected and have amazing roots in the landscape.

We may say what happened is long gone, but in reality, it lives on, and the suffering continues in much more subtle ways. We came to the Kimberley with certain goals in mind. So, what of that? Let's be completely honest here:

1. This year, we did not witness the same level of acute injury, wounds and conditions that are easily treated by first aid. We did treat people but not to the extent I thought we would. The health status, coincidently or not, seems to have improved and that's a great thing.

2. Chronic illnesses, however, remain. The disease burden in these friendly communities is huge and Australia should be ashamed that its own people and children are dying from treatable disease and their average lifespan is so much shorter. I will not list the health issues as I have mentioned them many times before and I am aware of the cultural pride in the communities that were so kind to Peggy and me.

3. Never in my wildest dreams did I think taking some balloons and a pump would provide so much joy and fun with children. The trip throughout the north-west is worth it, just for that. I am so glad I packed the stupid things.

4. In the planning phase of this trip, many people said, "Be careful up in the north! It's not safe for whitefellas and keep your stuff locked away." What complete bollocks! Despite unfounded anxiety in some towns, I never once have been threatened by blackfellas. I can't say the same about my own people. I was harassed, I was told off, I was made to feel unwelcome. The truth is they are the snakes in the grass, and they feel threatened by my presence and the friendships I developed.

So, there we have a little evaluation and some cursory conclusions, but 'it's not over till the fat lady sings'!

We leave Wyndham heading east to Kununurra, down the lovely new road to the port. This road is going to facilitate much of the export of gas, rare earth metals and livestock to China, etc. The new generations of batteries and cars will come to depend on the Kimberley and my hope is the prosperity trickles down to the Indigenous people who own this vast resource. I am not holding my breath, and neither are the Elders I spend time with.

We visit Kununurra War Memorial and I give Peggy a tub; we've got to keep up appearances, after all. Then, we head further east across ground we know so well.

Suddenly, it appears – the Argyle Dam – an immense lake created to irrigate the far north-west, an aquamarine ocean in the desert. Its capacity is 17 times that of Sydney Harbour, and it's a magnet for water lovers everywhere. There are huge houseboats, catamarans, and all manner of watercraft. Of course, it has many crocs in its deep dark depths, and we did see one from far away.

Argyle Lake is testament to humanity's abilities in altering entire landscapes and waterways. From the 300 metre plus dam wall, looking down on the river below is staggering in its enormity. The rock faces above the water in the dam are stained by the water levels. It is clear the dam is at low levels as the surface lies many metres lower than the pale tide mark. Riding through the martian landscapes and canyons that lead to this extraordinary result of human effort makes me feel very small.

Leaving this huge feature and bastion of the Grey Nomad, we get back onto the road home. We eventually reach the oasis of Timber Creek once again and I am gagging for a beer; it's so hot now for this old Pommy git. Tonight, we shall camp away from the river and return in the morning, possibly staying to meet the locals.

First, though, tonight I am treated to a little show by a delightful young singer at the Timber Creek Roadhouse called *Ali Jam Music*. That's also the name of her Facebook page, and I think worth checking out.

Darkness has well and truly fallen when Peggy and I ride back west to the campsite we set earlier. It's very hot under the mosquito net, but I am glad I have it because the buggers here have chainsaws!

DAY 36

In the morning at sunrise, we get a lovely view through the mesh. It doesn't take long to get going and I leave the camp as it is, and head into the settlement in search of coffee. Fuelled up, I'm ready to explore Timber Creek, a surprisingly important place, despite its remote location. We first ride up onto the escarpment overlooking this spectacular region and river.

We find the 'NACKEROOS' memorial, which commemorates the group of hardy soldiers sent to the far north in 1942 to watch and monitor for any Japanese activity. A difficult task in this environment, only made possible because Aboriginal trackers and guides helped them survive by finding water and bush tucker. Plaques tell of the sacrifice these men made, months on end in mosquito ridden swamps, tropical ulcers, diseases and being completely cut off from the world – hardy men indeed! On returning to normal lives in society, they were a lost and unruly bunch.

The views of the Victoria River valley and Timber Creek are just awesome as the bush and waterway extends into infinity. Having taken the photos I wanted, we ride down to the highway and over Victoria River on the Bradshaw Bridge, a huge, wide concrete structure capable of taking all manner of military vehicles and ending with massive steel gates. This is the entry to Bradshaw, one of Australia's most extensive live fire training areas where military exercises are conducted using all manner of weapons and ammunition, such as the Abrams tank and air warfare weapons. Not a good place to pick up 'that funny-looking object' – it might be a 'HEAT' or 'HESH' round that failed to detonate. The river here is, of course, a very dangerous place, hiding many large saltwater crocodiles. In one spot, we saw a large croc trap near the water's edge; camping near the water is not advised!

We go on to visit the Gregory Tree. In this place, an explorer called Augustus Gregory and his party made camp in 1856 whilst looking for timber to repair his damaged schooner, the *Tom Tough*. Whilst there, they made themselves immortal by carving the dates into a large boab tree by the river. It must have taken some time as the carving is deep and large.

Returning to Timber Creek, we stop off to visit the dry, burnt cemetery. Not many graves here but some are interesting, with headstones made of old relics and piles of rock. Life here was obviously tough as many commemorate the deaths of young people.

Back further east to the roadhouse, we meet a local Pastor, an 83-year-old Elder of some talent and tenacity. He was a stockman at Waterloo Station in his youth, but a horse fell on his leg whilst mustering cattle and it was permanently damaged. Not to be outdone, he became an Aboriginal Health Care Worker in the region as well as its Pastor. A hard man, he was getting frustrated with his leg. So, when he was evacuated to Darwin, he asked them to remove the offending appendage. He was so matter of fact about it! I guess when you have lived and worked in such extreme conditions with the handicap of a badly lame leg slowing you down, it's a small price to pay for comfort.

Everyone loves doggies and I miss mine. So, when a Grey Nomad turns up and gets out with three little Jack Russells, naturally I take pictures.

Tonight, after a meal, I will return to camp and get some sleep because tomorrow I head off again, this time for Katherine via the magnificent Victoria River settlement.

DAY 37

I am no expert, but Peggy Pegasus is, because she is 2,000 kilometres into her third lap of this enormous continent. She has learnt many things and thought she should pass them on!

HAVE YOU EVER THOUGHT, *I WANT TO DO THE BIG LAP*?

Well, just do it – throw on your swag and go! Here's some tips for beginners like me, as no one told me this stuff.

- Always travel with your lights on, as the roads are straight and long. By doing this, you 'announce your presence', especially to road trains.
- Get a USB charger. Keeping your phone or tablet charged whilst you ride is great.
- Using a cord, attach your keys to your tank bag, etc. and carry a spare set around your neck.
- Highway pegs. I made some highway pegs so that I could stretch my legs out on long hauls. I also padded them, allowing me to rest my

calves on them for dead straight knees. It works a treat.

- Loud horn. Essential, as most bike horns are too quiet; wildlife, trucks and cyclists get to hear you coming.

- Quality occy straps. Avoid cheap occy straps and ensure they will not fly back taking your eye out.

- Camming compression straps. I find these are brilliant; just thread through and pull tight, and everything is good and secure.

- Spare fuel can and nozzle. There are many long legs between fuel stops, and sometimes servos run out, so carry an extra can. And don't lose the nozzle, as I did.

- Keep weight over the rear axle. Cheap panniers, etc. can be found. I bought some watertight camera cases at Bunnings for $50 each. They are great. Loads too far back behind the rear axle make the front unstable. So, just light stuff in a top box (clothes, etc).

- First aid kit. I have two comprehensive, remote area kits because of the mission, but all that is needed is a simple motoring kit, available at most auto outlets, but don't forget a snake bite first aid kit.

- Knobby tyres. If you think you can ride the Big Lap (16,000 kilometres) all on tarmac, you are mistaken. You will end up in dirt at some stage, so good quality adventure tyres are a must.

- Oil changes. Do these frequently as oil gets hammered in the heat. I change oil every 3,000 kilometres and the filter every 6,000 kilometres has come out clean. And the donk's never missed a beat.
- Chain maintenance. Lubricate the drive chain every day at the end of a ride when it's warm and keep the tension as per the manual. You may need to clean it occasionally, especially in sand or muddy terrain.
- Tank bag and phone. Keep all those things you need quickly (wallet, phone, camera, compass, GPS, etc.) in a tank bag. Do not leave the phone in that cute, see-through vinyl pouch on the bag. In 40 plus degree sunshine, it will get cooked!
- Know your range. Watch your odometer and know how many kilometres range you have. The outback is not a good place to run out of petrol.
- Side stand. Use a plate on the side stand or you may find your steed lying in the dirt or sand. I had one welded to Peggy and it's a godsend at times.

On the road from Katherine to Daly Waters, temperatures are getting hot. So, after arriving in Katherine, fuelling up and getting rations, it's to the RSL club to get a beer to the "...back of the neck, Mr C."

Outside the RSL, I see an anti-tank recoilless gun with its venturi clearly showing. These weapons were a major threat to tanks later in WW2. They fired 'HESH' and 'HEAT' rounds very accurately at the enemy and almost made tanks obsolete. Highly mobile and quickly set up, they could kill tanks before they were spotted. First one I've seen since leaving the Army. We were still using them until the 1980s. New reactive and chobham armours have made the modern tank impervious to such weapons.

Enough of that. Peggy and I set off south through the red-hot centre and find a good roadside campsite at dinner time. So, we stop and set up for the night. The evening is very hot again, but fortunately it cools once the sun drops below the horizon.

A restless night follows; traffic is heavy till late. There are loads of road trains, as wildlife on the road does not worry these land-locked leviathans.

DAY 38

On rising, it's straight to the stove for coffee; I need that caffeine hit in the morning. Strike camp and onto Mataranka, an interesting place in the NT, set in the limestone lens, great karst scenery. This vast aquifer runs all the way south from Katherine, a source of the purest water in the region rising to the surface in caves and pools. It has shaped all the surface rocks, creating weird landscapes and waterholes.

A visit to the local thermal pools is called for. I need a natural bath and it's truly lovely there. Set in native palms, these pools are part of the Barkly Aquifer. The water flows through at 130 litres per second at about 28 degrees. As with most water in karst geology, it is crystal and has a slightly sulphurous pong, but it's great. There are plenty of freshwater crocs and turtles, but leave them alone and you will be fine. My swim is excellent, but I've probably polluted the water with my stink! Local people here are really worried about proposed fracking for gas that runs the risk of killing the aquifer and source of water for many. Go figure! Our governments of all persuasions seem quite happy to allow this to go ahead!

After leaving this little oasis, which I thoroughly recommend as not much is free these days, we go into Mataranka to do our washing and rehydrate. I was, however, eaten alive by the native mosquitos that exist in abundance around the pools.

Mataranka is an enigma; so much is expected but when you arrive, it is just a plain looking street, with a couple of fibro roadhouses and a very run-down pub. People sit in groups across the road in the shade of big native trees on green grass watching the world pass them by.

Once the dirty deeds are done, we leave to head to Daly Waters. We've had enough of the famous Daly Waters Pub for this trip. There are too many caravans there this time, although it's a lovely stop over. So, this time we're off to the Highway Inn Roadhouse, a nice spot with good hospitality, food (and loads of it), and several pretty Irish girls serving. Bangers and mash tonight is a treat – much nicer than stewed steak and beans from a tin, hey ho!

One of my cardinal rules in the outback is not to 'primitive camp' near a roadhouse or any place where people gather. I look for evidence of parties: bottles, cans and such. I break this rule tonight and camp in an old waste dump area 200 metres from the roadhouse.

All's good till about midnight when all hell breaks loose. Cars, V8s, 4x4 hoons are doing drunken doughnuts within metres of my tent and Peggy. Fires are lit and plenty of grog is being drunk, and it goes on for hours. Of course, we keep quiet, lights out, etc., but it's a sleepless night. My fear is getting run over by a wayward Landcruiser driven by a drunken hoon. All's well that ends well, as we are not seen, and are left alone.

Continuing on a theme, I think (seeing as I taught Outdoor Education for 40 odd years), a few tips on motorcycle camping may be useful to those who are contemplating a long ride through the top end of a big lap around the country. Just a few basics. I hope I'm not teaching those experienced how to suck eggs!

- Modern stoves are just amazing! My little beauty only weighs 65 grams and works better than anything I've had in the past.
- Billies come complete and slide inside each other with the stove, taking little room and weighing sweet FA.
- Wet bags are essential. I stuff my tent, my fly, my sleeping bag in one, dirty clothes also. It takes no time at all to strike camp when you use these.
- A good sleep mat or folding bed makes for a better rest. Mine is self-inflating and about 7cm thick when full, which is easily done.

- A self-inflating pillow.
- Baby wipes or bath cloths take up little room and allow you to freshen up in the morning, getting all those important areas (if you know what I mean).
- A magnetic light to stick on the sickle or a convenient post.
- Anything easy for nourishment; dried food is good also, but you will need to carry extra water. I only carry enough tinned food for between roadhouses as they are heavy. Best are the ring pull tins, Pareto's Principle being the general guideline.
- Carry enough water at all times, and a little in the bottom of a billy prior to cooking food stops its sticking and burning.
- All water is suitable if it's clear and boiled for a couple of minutes.
- The tent fly is a good mosquito net. In the dry season, nothing more is needed, and it lets air circulate.
- Spray inside the net before entering, getting rid of any mozzies that snuck in.
- Campfires are nice, but unnecessary. One can get out of hand as it's tinder dry here.
- Sneakers for camping; have bare feet and you will get hurt.

DAY 39

In the morning, the usual strike camp – in full view of the remaining revellers, to their surprise! We go over to the roadhouse for a coffee and a bite. Onto the Stuart Highway for the long straight and boring ride south, past Elliott, another of those sad places in our amazing country that has featured in a documentary called *Utopia* by John Pilger. The report documents, with passion, the truth about unjust poor health and conditions in which many Indigenous people are forced to live.

We stop here for a break from the monotonous drone of Peggy's knobby tyres on the long, straight, hot road. This brings me to my last, brief piece of advice on travelling the country by motorsickle, especially the far north:

- DON'T RIDE AT NIGHT! The critters love the warm road, and you do not want to get into a scrap with a water buffalo!

Always be aware of the stock and wildlife. Cattle

stations are largely unfenced, and massive cattle wander freely. Remember, I saw an almost two-ton Brahman Bull hit by a car at 110 kilometres per hour near Warmun in the Kimberley. The car was totalled and the driver very lucky to survive. Adjust your speed, scan the road well ahead, attract attention with your horn well in advance of critters, horses, camels, eagles, cattle and so on. Remember they can, and do, change direction!

If, like me, you are riding a bike that is flat out at 80kph fully loaded, (like the postie bikes I bumped into), then be assertive on the road and use your mirrors constantly. I have found the left hand side of the road to be the puncture zone. There's lots of debris, potholes and dead wildlife attracting scavengers.

Also, if you are on the left, many Grey Nomads think, '*Oh! I can just squeeze through*', and they know how thick the paint is on their caravan! Don't give them a chance! The crown of your lane is often oily and slippery with bits and bobs from trucks and cars. So, I avoid that position also.

I ride in the right-hand side-wheel tracks, but not so close to the white lines (if there are any) to be in a head-on risk. This way, if you use your mirrors and see an approaching baby boomer, you control the situation. When it's safe, signal clearly and move left. This gives you a good clearance and safety zone. Plus, they appreciate the move. Only allow an overtake if you think it is safe, as you still have the upper hand and buffer zone. Once they pass, flash your lights, wave and get out of the puncture zone.

Road trains! These things do 110 kilometres an hour in the Red Centre and take a while to pass. I have found these drivers very courteous and aware of the responsibility they have driving a huge beast with four long trailers and prime mover. When you see one, the same principle as for caravans applies; they generally only pass when it is safe. Move left, slow down a little, look straight ahead (not at the side of the truck, as that will scare you to death). Be aware the rear trailer may swing a little and as soon as it is clear, give the driver an unambiguous signal it's safe to move over. Do not sit behind these things. If there's something up front in the road, he may just drive over it, but it will bring you down. During our five months of lapping, Peggy has only overtaken one road train and it was slow. Make sure the road is clear ahead for miles.

As for approaching road trains, give them a wide berth, and also move left. The blast wave can be hot and huge; best avoided. Again signal your intent – the drivers of these big rigs love it when you save them hassle and washing off their speed; it takes a while, many gears and fuel to get road trains rolling.

Some of this will be irrelevant to riders of big, fast, adventure bikes who can pass a road train safely. My advice there is to smoke 'em and get

away from all other vehicles, including my generation with the living room, bedroom, kitchen and
bathroom in tow!

Stay alert! It's hot – very hot – so take plenty of
breaks. And stay hydrated.

After departing Elliott, Peggy and I are out of
contact for a while. On leaving, we encounter a
huge convoy of road trains snaking its way north
carrying mining equipment. I'm glad we never had
to try passing this circus load of wheel and steel.

The Northern Territory and Stuart Highway
has a series of great free campsites on the roads.
They are little more than large laybys, but they
have water, tables and covered areas. We decide
to spend the night at Attack Creek as we've been
here before. So, pulling off the road at about 1500
hours, we locate a spot near a tank and table, setting
up quickly. I find these places useful and amusing
because at about 1530 hours, the Grey Nomads in
their big rigs turn up.

There is a ritual to be followed by these extreme
adventurers, and (for many) it goes like this:

1. Enter the layby like meat ants swarming over
    a dead camel. Do a couple of laps trying to
    find your own spot as far away from any other
    nomad as possible, which of course is 'fooking'
    impossible.
2. The wifey gets out and proceeds to direct hubby
    in reversing the rig into a tight space. This

invariably ends up in conflict where the hubby repeatedly gets in and out to check the wife's commands are correct, lest he reverses into the log boundary. I love this bit; I wouldn't miss it for quids.

3. Once satisfied all is in order, the wifey gets back in the 4x4 into the aircon and waits whilst her man lowers the levelling legs and gets the van stable and level.

4. Once happy, the wifey gets in the van, never to be seen again, and starts pottering around. Footsteps and the noise of cupboards and pumps to fill the kettle fill the air.

5. Then comes the setting up of the Satellite Antenna; this must be perfect and Mr 'Frank Incredits' is very fussy to get the television picture perfect, not wanting to spoil Netflix or the footy viewing. Then comes the setup of the waste hose for the sink and washing machine; wifey starts washing with accompanying noise.

6. Hubby then enters the mansion on wheels; on goes the aircon and generator to charge the batteries.

7. That is the last you will see of this species of nomadic homo sapiens, but due to thin walls you will hear the couple banging about, somewhat like the noise hamsters make scurrying around in their box and on the exercise wheel. Of course, the footy or Netflix is always there

for everyone else to enjoy – so considerate of them to let the whole camp place listen in!

8. That's it. They will be seen no more, unless their shitter is full, and they must slum it!

9. SOMETIMES, IT IS ALL TOO MUCH! Mr 'Frank Incredits' and Ms 'Dee Mingrates' get frustrated and just leave, as they realise they are not the only extreme outdoors people touring OZ!

10. If you are a Grey Nomad ... sorry! It's only satire.

DAY 40

In the morning, I wake to a strong, cool wind blowing across the road and camp. It's not cold but I need my coffee. So, I set up the stove and heat the water to enjoy the caffeine lift. Striking camp is routine: everything is stuffed into the wet bag and personal items into the tank bag. Then, we hit the road before the hamsters are even filling their cheek pouches with bacon and eggs.

South to Three Ways and a quick stop to fuel up. In the roadhouse we are served by a delightful, attractive woman from Berlin. She is in her mid-forties and has the most engaging personality and haunting blue-grey eyes. I fall in love AGAIN!

I digress. After one more coffee and bacon roll, Peggy and I are on the road south again, and on ground not yet covered on this trip. Soon, we are in Tennant Creek.

I see the Tennant Creek Hotel, which is closed at this time of the morning, but it reminds me of last year when I was dying for a beer, having ridden over 300 kilometres in the heat. I boldly walked into the pub on that occasion. It was like that scene from the bar in *Star Wars*: I was the only whitefella in the place, which was packed out and noisy, with shouting, talking and a fight at the back.

Then, BOOM! Deadly silence. All those people stopped and looked at me. I felt like a spare prick at a wedding! Once the barmaid returned from busting up the fight, I confidently ordered a beer. Then, everything seemed to reanimate. Everyone either ignored or accepted me, striking up friendly conversations and curiosity about Peggy parked just outside. I drank my ale, said goodbye to my new acquaintances and left.

Back to real time, Peggy and I did our customary visit to the town's war memorial and took pictures. Leaving town, the cross wind is howling, bending tall palms over and making my left shoulder ache, fighting the steering. Further down the highway, we spot a satellite dish that has a slot in which to place your mobile phone or tablet. Like magic, in the middle of the desert I can phone friends and even check Facebook. The marvels of technology!

Presently, we are at the Devils Marbles Hotel having coffee. These geological features here are truly enigmatic, formed 350 million years ago as bedrock granite that has since been cracked, jointed, exfoliated and been subjected to ice wedging, resulting in these curious landforms, like massive snooker balls perched on top of each other spread over a red earth table. They really do look like they have been thrown, balanced and fractured by a force not of our world.

I go to the Devils Marbles camp tonight. I want to see their character metamorphose in the changing light of a Red Centre sunset. I want to see them at sunrise. However, we first pop into the pub 12 kilometres down the road for a couple of beers before returning to the swag. We are served by two stunning American girls. It's a great spot; if you are in the NT you must visit.

The actual campsite is, as you would expect, very popular. Satellite dishes take root very quickly and the 1530 mobile township arrives on time, with the usual fun and games. A very brave lady, rolls up in her little car with her bubby. We get talking straight away. She is on the long trip to Alice, to join her ranger husband who has just landed a job in the parks down that way. I am surprised when she asks me to look after and entertain her wee son whilst she erects her tent. I am pleased to do both. He is a gorgeous wee man, easy to please and happy to laugh and chuckle at this silly old Boomer. I have a good time, but in the end, she needs help because the ground is basically granite and tent pegs have no chance. I showed her how to use rocks as an anchor because the south easterly wind is howling. All good; we get her sorted.

A young Frenchman called Jeremy (not the British Officer type – he did not have a speech defect or shooting stick), is riding a Honda 125 (Jennifer) across the country to Cairns. He quizzes me for advice, which I happily give. Then, he rides off with Camooweal Queensland as his next stop. What a valiant effort!

A reasonably good night is had at the camp: some live guitar playing, shenanigans and laughter from the gathered nomads is followed by the peace of the central desert.

Even the wind drops!

DAY 41

Reveille, and back comes the breeze which, in the desert, is quite cold. Packing up camp along with Peggy and me are the young mother and her little baby. He is well wrapped in blankets and in his bouncing seat, happy to dole out heartening smiles to a silly old man. Not much to do; our routine is set in now. So, 'Rev up and fook off!' as we used to say in the Army.

Onto the roadhouse 12 kilometres south for coffee, a sandwich and another flirt with the American girls. I take some photos of two huge Tonka truck tippers destined for the mines. They are the enormous completely autonomous trucks they use there – NO DRIVERS!

Leaving the roadhouse, riding is tiring because the massive crosswind has picked up. So, we aim to reach the remote little community and little shack and fuel stop at Barrow Creek. They have a repeater station there, so I am able to post yesterday's blog, and take a break from the easterly gales. Some children arrive, and as if by magic,

Mr Balloon turns up and entertains them for 30 minutes or so.

Then it's on to Tea Tree where we will camp somewhere yet unknown. On the way, we cross The Ghan railway line that connects Adelaide to the far north and Darwin, a long rail journey indeed. It's not something I could cope with, but I'm happy to take pictures of the rails to infinity.

At the present moment, we are at the Tea Tree Roadhouse just chillin' and writing the blog. A few guys turn up on bikes, having crossed the desert and Birdsville track. One is riding a 1974 BMW 750 S – good on him. He's hit a huge rock and the rim on the classic is barely functional, but (as with these stalwart riders), he keeps on going.

Now, I am going to purchase some rations for tonight and breakfast tomorrow, then find a good sleeping spot. I saw a reasonable site five kilometres back at the cemetery. I do not believe in ghosts or God, but I will let you know in the morning.

I meet the lovely Mariah from Wollongong in the roadhouse. She explains she was not named after Mariah Carey, as the diva was not famous when she was born 25 years ago. I have a little chuckle to myself, thinking Mariah Carey has whiskers and has been around as long as Methuselah. But never mind, she's a lovely girl, nonetheless.

Refreshed and renewed, Peggy and I get on the road to our camp, not far down the highway. As we're speeding along, my right-hand mirror shatters and falls off into the road. Thirty thousand kilometres of vibration has broken the mounting bracket. NOT HAPPY, JAN! I really need this mirror to see approaching road trains and nomads. However, I keep going to camp.

On arrival, it's on with the billy and coffee, before the hordes of hamsters arrive in their little aluminium boxes.

I think about it a little and pull off the left-hand mirror, which strangely has an opposite thread, and figure out a way to replace the broken one. It works fine, and I still have the left-hand stalk for the USB charger. The problem's solved! I am happy; the image in the mirror is left-handed and inverted, but I can cope with that! (I laugh out loud).

I'm putting up camp, getting settled, when the nomads start to arrive. So, I think I will take a little walk around the site. I soon notice one of the caravans looks like it is being attacked by a rare 'Black Banded Boomer snake' but it is simply the waste pipe pumping crap into the desert. I keep my distance but take considerable risks to get a photo of the offending five metre plastic 'reptile'.

Then, I notice another natural wonder: a round raised donut-shaped pile of soil and twigs. Is it the nest of the endangered Uranus Bird? It used to be common in these parts, until an epidemic of Avian Haemorrhoids nearly wiped them out. I have no idea where the name 'Uranus Bird' came from, possibly the shape?

Enough of the natural history lesson – I'm no Attenborough!

I'm hungry, so I slice up some cheese kransky, add it to some beans, heat it and have some tucker. Later, the evening gets cool, as it does in Central Desert country. I light a small fire and sit pondering the universe. I notice one Grey Nomad has a scooter on the back of his van instead of towing another car or 4x4, as some do. I ask him, "What's it for?"

He rather rudely tells me, "When my missus is nagging and giving me the shits, I make her ride the fooker behind the van."

Not nice really, but there you have it.

So, with that interesting snippet of boomer life, I go to my swag and quickly fall asleep.

DAY 42

I wake in the morning, dreaming of hamsters or gerbils for some reason. Then, I realise I just need to go to the dunny. Strange how the bowels can play tricks on you; quite nice though.

The sunrise is in the East, I think? Either way, it's stunning and I get a photo. And then I start out for the Alice.

I ride a short distance to a place called Aileron. I don't know the origin of the name, but I am not going to get into a FLAP about it – BOOM BOOM! It's the way I tell 'em. They also have a dunny with a view – a very good one for anyone that wants to watch you on the loo. A little too Teutonic for my tastes.

Outside the roadhouse, there are some fascinating large statues of proud warriors from happier times for Indigenous people.

By now, you might be thinking, '*Why would changing the mirrors invert the image...*'

Leaving Aileron on the stretch to the civilisation of Alice Springs – a boring ride with The Ghan railway to my left, desert scrub to my right and a vanishing point in front – we reach the Tropic of Capricorn, leaving the tropics behind and entering the temperate regions of the southern hemisphere. Funny, though, I don't even notice the temperature change when I step back and forth across the line. Those cartographers are full of shit!

I am going to have a couple of days off here, staying with a friend whilst I recharge my batteries. But first, we will be tourists and wait, because he already has a guest.

We ride up ANZAC Hill, the ascent lined with beautifully cut steel memorials to each of the campaigns Australia has fought in, starting with the Crimea and last, the present involvements in Middle East and Afghanistan. At the summit overlooking the town, is an impressive obelisk with the words 'LEST WE FORGET'. We still do, but nonetheless it's a great tribute to the fallen. Even more touching is the First Nations flag flying high and proud as Peggy poses for her photo.

Our descent into Alice proper takes us to the local Yamaha dealer. I'm trying to source another left-hand mirror for Peggy. These people are mega helpful, a lovely lady taking me into their storeroom as she searches through a bin of spare parts off wrecked bikes. We locate a mirror similar but in chrome, and as it looks like the correct thread, I go outside and find it fits perfectly. Peggy is happy because she now has both eyes in the back of her head again. The lady said she is so impressed by Peggy's stamina we can have it for free! A big thanks to Yamaha of Alice Springs.

From there, we go to find some amber nectar and end up at Todd Tavern. I'm sitting quietly when a local Elder approaches me, selling a painting. Now, I am not particularly fond of dot paintings as they are not to my taste, but this is essentially a landscape. I love landscape paintings and am immediately taken by it. I am the worst at haggling but think I will give it a try.

I say, "How much?"

The gentleman says, "A hundred dollars."

I think, *Right, I've got this bloke.* "I will give you seventy dollars."

He says, "One hundred."

Not to be deterred, I try again. "Eighty dollars."

He looks at me with a gleam in his dark eyes and says, "One hundred dollars!"

I am beaten; in the words of Monty Python, *'This bloke won't haggle.'*

After a couple refreshing schooners of angel's piss, we leave Alice, buy some rations and return to the Tropic of Capricorn to camp another night. We are getting set up when a 4x4 from the remote Yipirinya School arrives. They are interested in Peggy; she's such a flirt and has been recently scrubbed up in a local wash (got to keep up appearances). Mr Balloon is onto it, providing some amusement and frivolity for the children. It's good fun.

Then, another young traveller arrives, and we start a conversation again about Peggy. She breaks the ice at parties. We speak into the night, and he tells me of his battles with depression and how he is travelling to find meaning. I tell him of my own fight with PTSD and being hospitalised. I cannot give him answers, because the Dark Canine is always there, waiting. The Black Dog never rests, but he can be appeased by focusing on helping others. Eventually, we both retire under a now cooling and clear night sky.

DAY 43

In the central desert of Australia, it can be 45 plus degrees during the day but often, with no insulating cloud, it's close to zero in the morning. That's the case now – once I strike camp and say goodbye to my new brother, it's a very chilly ride to Alice and breakfast with my mate Mick. My favourite – Eggs Benedict. Yummy, with real hollandaise!

We return to his place, where I'm able to get a proper shower and shave. I have no idea how anyone can tolerate a beard permanently; they are filthy things! Anyway, it's gone for a while. A snooze is in order, so both Mick and I get some shut eye (in separate rooms, before any of my mates start being smart)!

Rested, I get dressed and head into town for a little look around, window shopping and a schooner. Alice is enigmatic. A modern town, stuck in the middle of bone-dry desert with huge temperature extremes, surrounded by massive rock ridges and aquamarine skies.

Peggy and I return to Mick's, and she is now resting gently in the shade. I love her! And for the first time in six weeks, I get to sleep in a bed. It's great!

DAY 44

I wake up at dawn, well rested, thanks to Mick. After we have brekkie, Peggy wants to do the tourist thing around the region, so her fans can enjoy her travels. First thing I notice about Alice is the surrounding escarpments and the access gaps that allow entry to its flat centre.

We ride out to Simpsons Gap, a spectacular ravine straight through a red precipitous sandstone escarpment towering up on either side of a ten-metre wide sandy, dry, riverbed. The McDonnell Ranges leave me in no doubt this whole area was once a shallow sea. The evidence lies in the consistent rock strata that has been uplifted and folded by massive geological forces. When I examine the layers, I clearly see compressed sand and mudstones that have been plasticised by heat and pressure over billions of years.

Rivers have cut swathes through these landforms, creating the basin we know as Alice Springs. Any notion the Earth is only 6,000 years old, or that man walked the earth with dinosaurs, seems crazy in the light of such proof. Wandering through the canyon, we see rock wallabies jumping and hiding in the gaps of a huge broken rock fall; these curious creatures are also interested in us.

We leave the ranges and ride back through Alice to the Stuart Highway and the start of tomorrow's journey to South Australia. Peggy remembers the Old Ghan train from our last visit and insists on a photo opportunity with the rusting hulk in the desert.

Afterwards, we ride to the Australian Museum of Transport, where we find trucks, cars and motorcycles from the past which have been lovingly restored. I have always admired those who allow us to see our grandparents' past; they do humanity a great service bringing to life times that would be forgotten.

Tonight, Mick and I are going to the local Golf Club for dinner. I am looking forward to that before continuing the 3,000 kilometre trip to my mountain home via Port Augusta and Broken Hill and seeing my dogs (especially my whippet puppy, Loretta; missing her heaps). At the golf club, it's such a paradox to see beautiful greens and fairways in the midst of a desert; all watered, of course, from underground aquifers. Let's not mess with the earth's natural springs, for example by fracking. I'm really enjoying my stay here.

DAY 45

In the Alice, you do notice the very high numbers of First Australians throughout the town, and whilst doing the shopping, I also noticed that the region has a large, dedicated police presence, especially outside bottle shops. Three police officers remain vigilant to the purchase of take-away alcohol, ID is always required, and the purchase of large amounts raise suspicion and create many checks and balances. Mick explains to me this is a direct result of alcohol abuse, crime and domestic violence. He seems to be understandably ambivalent regarding the efficacy of the laws, but says domestic violence seems to be down, and that's a good thing.

This journey has been a huge learning curve for me, meeting as I have so many First Australians and Elders. I have no answers to these intractable issues; for me they are far too complex for simplistic solutions. In these situations, I tend to put my 'Alien Head' on and imagine what a space traveller watching with an impartial mind would think.

My thoughts wander to 60,000 plus years of human history here in Australia. Having served many countries as a young soldier, I do know the problem is similar for Indigenous peoples around the planet: North America, Canada, South America, Africa, Alaska. Coincidence? I think not.

It seems to me, wherever Abrahamic cultures invade and spread around our planet, the different cultures clash, with ours expecting assimilation. My friend, Russ, has studied this phenomenon. It's not a matter of who's right or wrong; more an issue of Indigenous people having lived with their environment for many thousands of years, taking only what they need and developing technologies that match the survival needs of the group. Why invent a wheel or gun if you don't need one? Pareto's Principle applies. This principle argues that 80% of the results of effort come from the first 20% of that effort. If you want to achieve the remaining 20% of results, then you will need to work 80% harder!

Australian Aboriginals maintained this sustainable living for 60,000 years and more – and built the oldest man-made structures on our planet. They baked bread 25,000 years before the Egyptians! We think of 200 years of Australian history in the light of European economic and moral values. As for economic and technological growth – can we really expect assimilation from such proud, innovative and resourceful peoples in less than 200 years?

Indigenous peoples have a long oral history and

connection with their land and kin. Can we really use the word 'SORRY' to compensate for the thousands of massacres, rapes, dispossessions, diseases and discriminations?

Having spent time with such eminent leaders and Elders, such as Reginald Birch, OAM and Indigenous advocate to such bodies as the United Nations, I don't think we can. I have no idea what reparations may appease historical wrongs, but Mr Birch in his conversations with me was pessimistic and believes we are witnessing the creeping genocide of his people in the Kimberley and worldwide. It is high time to recognise First Australians in law and give them their own voice in our constitution and parliament.

In the light of these truths, should we be surprised that the same issues of substance abuse, crime and violence that exist in our culture are issues for other dispossesed Indigenous people worldwide? *Once Were Warriors*, a powerful movie about the proud Mauri peoples of New Zealand, springs to mind. It depicts how they, too, struggle with European settlement and discrimination.

OK, enough of my mental musings – back to Peggy and me. The journey south continues with the first stop at Stuarts Well for some refreshments. There is a camel farm nearby and some curious emus approach us. A natural spring exists here, creating a pond, no doubt the source of the name and an oasis for weary camel trains throughout the decades.

We don't stay long here as our goal today is Erl-dunda, the intersection of the Stuart and Lasseter Highways. It is the turn-off to Uluru (Ayers Rock) which Peggy and I visited last year. It was a long excursion.

In 2019, MP Pauline Hanson attempted to climb the rock in order to demonstrate her opposition to its closure for climbers and her support for individual freedoms in Australia. Unable to get no more than 40 metres up, she sat down, crying and in total terror. It seems the spirits of the ancestors did not want such a nasty individual on this sacred ground. Me? I just thought it was hilarious karma.

We reach Erldunda in good time and spy a campsite for tonight in the bush nearby. So, we set up our little bush camp down the road north from Erldunda. Peggy and I are treated to an event I have not recorded in the Red Centre before. Looking out to our east over the scrub and red dirt, the full moon is rising in all its supermoon orange glory. Out to our west, the sun is setting as only it does in Australia: fiery burning amber. It never gets dark tonight. We are in the land of the midnight moon; not a good time for infantry to conduct a section attack, as everything was as clear as day.

DAY 46

In the morning at sunrise, we get the same nature's light show. The moon is setting in the west and the sun is rising in the east. Both celestial bodies are just peeping over their respective horizons at exactly the same time. It's an event I have never seen before, but I guess common in this desert, and photos just don't do it justice.

Once finished with the light show I start Peggy's faithful beating heart and we roll out of the dust on our way back to Erldunda for lifegiving coffee and breakfast. It's fun there; a lovely hostess gives me a free coffee, so naturally Mr Balloon becomes active, making the staff some latex memories. The hostess says, "You have just made my day!" Silly things, eh? Then a little family from China becomes Mr Balloon's next customers. Their little girl is just gorgeous, all smiles and so thrilled with her balloon puppy. To tell the truth, these little random acts of kindness and senseless beauty makes mine and Peggy's day.

I fill Peggy with go-juice and off down the road to Kulgera, only ninety kilometres away. Peggy reaches a landmark of 36,000 kilometres. That's 4000 kilometres over a double lap of our continent! We stop at Kulgera Roadhouse for a drink and some happy snaps. This world is so small; my friend Di in Canberra, actually knows the owner. He is so surprised when I say, "Hello from Di!" He's full of questions about her wellbeing, which I happily answer.

We leave Kulgera in good spirits heading south to the border of South Australia. There are only two more states to cross before we reach my house-sitter, Anthony, and my puppies at home. What I find intriguing about Australia is that when crossing some borders, the landscape changes immediately. This is the case as you enter South Australia – the rocky outcrops and termite mounds are replaced by flat, featureless desert and scrub. On the way we travel for a long time next to a massive goods train until it picks up speed and leaves us behind. It must be a kilometre long!

Travelling further we see a car stopped in the desert and a man waving us down. We pull up and he explains he has run out of petrol. The car is rundown, with broken windows and windscreen. We help him as much as we can and tell him we will let someone know he is stuck. As we leave him, I wonder if he will get help but twelve kilometres down the road, we see a police car and pull over to tell him the tale. He is going that way so at least the Indigenous gentleman is not stuck for too long.

We are now sitting at the Marla Roadhouse and plan to stay behind some piles of gravel at the south end. It's a good spot and despite the road trains playing music as they pass over a xylophone cattle grid, I sleep really well. It becomes reassuring after a while.

Tomorrow we head for Coober Pedy, the opal capital of Australia and somewhere I enjoyed last year thanks to some lovely blackfella mates we made. I hope they are there this year.

DAY 47

Last night's camp is easy to pack up and I'm over to the roadhouse for breakfast and coffee, served by the lovely waitress with a smile to die for and an attitude to match. Mr Balloon makes the young beauty an orange flower and, in return, she creates a flower on my coffee foam. It's great to be greeted by such positive, hardworking young people in the outback rest spots.

Outside, Peggy and I are met by a one-legged hardman from Hervey Bay. This stalwart guy has just climbed Uluru, not an easy thing on two legs, let alone one! He then drank beer from the prosthesis in celebration, quite a character. He lost his leg as a young man in an industrial accident but has not let that hold him back. Explanations and stories are exchanged; never let the truth stand in the way of a good story, eh?

Today's goal is to reach the famous opal mining town of Coober Pedy, so I throw my leg over Peggy and hit the road south again. First stop is Cadney Homestead, the gateway to Australia's 'Painted

Desert', a place of multi-coloured sand dunes and landforms. There I meet the most stunning Yorkshire lass from Doncaster. We recognise each other as 'Yorkshire Folk' immediately, speaking of the green and pleasant land and holidays in my hometown of Bridlington. The subject drifts onto fish and chips, an old Yorkshire favourite. Funnily we both agree that Australian fish and chips will never compare with those cooked in beef dripping in Yorkshire. It's official: Aussie *fush and chups* are a poor substitute. With that and a lovely smile I'm prompted to make the lovely lass a white swan balloon. I leave with a "Na then, lass," and a loud, "Rock on, Tommy!" You have to be Yorkshire to get that. Then we hit the road to Coober Pedy.

The Cadney region is famous for its wedge tailed eagles. These majestic raptors soar the thermals over a desert strewn with spinifex grass and rocks, forever looking for carrion by the roadside. With a two metre plus wingspan and dark plumage, their bird of prey beauty is almost equal to that of a Golden Eagle.

Approaching Coober Pedy some hundred kilometres later, the landscape becomes dotted with many small hillocks of white overburden from one metre mineshafts drilled into the desert. They look like piles of salt tipped there by some giant messing around at the table. Many skeletal machines lie around, mechanical T-Rex dinosaurs for sorting the spoil dug from narrow deep shafts that lie in wait for the unwary tourist. As the sign there says, 'Don't walk backwards!'

Amazingly we pass another Pegasus Royal Enfield heading north and give it a wave. There's only 50 of them in the country; what's the chance of two being on the same remote desert highway?

Peggy and I arrive in this very dusty and windy mining town of Coober Pedy. It looks like a wasteland from a science fiction movie but has a charm all its own. You can almost feel the 'Opal Fever' in this desert community. It is everywhere but no one looks rich; in fact, they're quite the opposite. I think it must be a struggle to mine this gemstone. The lack of water here is striking. All water requires an additional cost. For example, coin feed showers and stand pipes for caravans at a premium, costing more than beer.

DRINK BEER!

I like this frontier town and the hardman nature of the men and women that risk it all, gambling that they may find the illusive opal, which has no real use but to adorn our bodies in crystal rainbow jewellery that dances like fire in the light. I will explore more of the strange moonscape tomorrow.

Things happen in threes they say. Well, let's hope I'm done!

First, an overly sharp pull on a spanner results in a slip, and spanner rash. I knew it was going to happen, but I still do it.

Second, poor old Peggy is attacked this evening!

A mentally ill lady pushes her over, off her centre stand. Peggy crashes to the ground heavily. In keeping with her tank badge, *MADE LIKE A GUN*, the damage is minor, thankfully. It could have been far worse. Had it been my BMW, it would have led to thousands of dollars in repairs. I don't think the lady meant to hurt her. She seems angry and confused while people are shouting at her and telling me to call the cops. I spoke to her gently and she is so afraid of the cops, I would not have called them anyway. She's just another lost soul in our harsh world.

Third, I go to my swag, and I hear a snap. Glasses broken into two pieces! Bugger! I reach for my backup set. Snap! They break in two also. In the final words of the bushranger, Ned Kelly, 'Such is life!'

I try to get some sleep, before I fix them in the morning. Coober Pedy, however, is a noisy place at night. There is shouting, 4x4 doors slamming and people roaming around. Finally, the bliss of oblivion kicks in.

DAY 48

I wake at dawn to the sound of crows having a domestic. Completing the morning ablutions and SSS on rising, I pack the swag and go to the local roadhouse for some epoxy resin to fix the specs. I sit drinking coffee while gluing one set and taping the other to get the best result. The Araldite wins hands down, a temporary fix but at least I can see again.

The road south to Glendambo is blocked at the moment due to live rocket fire practice by the defence force at Woomera. This leaves me time to write up the blog and go to investigate the opal mining techniques and machines.

Opal, the gemstone, takes about five to six million years to form, as a result of water seeping down through sedimentary rocks rich in silica. Carbonic acid in the water dissolves and picks up the silica in solution. The solution eventually becomes saturated and can enter small voids in the rock and may crystalise out, forming the colourful crystalline patterns we see in good opal. Sometimes there is a fossil in the mudstones: a bone or shell. The solution will opalise the structure. These are very rare and valuable. Each of the opal displays I take a photo of is worth well over $100,000. Set these pieces in gold and you understand opal fever. My own piece of raw opal is something I treasure. It has a special value to me, reminding me of my friend, Marc, and his son who died as a very young man. I love the way it plays the light when I'm looking through it.

These determined and obsessed people use a big drill to bore down through the soft sedimentary mudstone and sand. The shaft is little more than a metre across but can be thirty metres deep. From its base, the miners work sideways across the layers hoping to pick up a vein of opal, most times unsuccessfully and so drill another shaft. The area is literally covered in them. Also strangely, Coober Pedy has an extremely high missing persons rate, and one wonders why...

The opal bearing rock crumbles easily and is sent to the surface where it is put through a huge truck mounted blower that blows off the dust and soil into a suspended big drum, from which it falls into a conical pile on the earth. Any solid matter containing opal drops out early, to be examined by the miners. Leases are guarded ferociously. Any unauthorised 'noodling' often results in conflict. It's a serious business living and working down a hole.

Speaking of living in a hole, many of the townsfolk dig their home in the rock and live in the cool environment underground. Rumour has it the

Underground Hotel here was paid for by the opal found as giant machines dug out the rooms and corridors, giving the structure an unearthly atmosphere consistent with the wrecked remains of the spacecraft, sitting just outside in the car park, from *The Chronicles of Riddick*, a 2004 science-fiction action movie filmed here starring Vin Diesel.

I will not make the 254 kilometre ride to the next roadhouse at Glendambo this evening, so I've bought some rations, water, coffee and chocolate for this evening's lonely roadside camp. I will head for Glendambo in the morning. Peggy's rear tyre is reaching its use by date, and I must reach civilisation for a new one.

DAY 49

After a fairly dramatic and challenging stay in Coober Pedy, Peggy and I take off south towards Glendambo knowing we may be stopped. The RAAF Bombing range is active, and the entire highway south can be closed for obvious safety reasons. After about fifty kilometres of bland road bordered by opal spoil mounds, we hit a roadblock. An RAAF officer dressed in a blue combat uniform (that's akin to putting a top hat on a cockroach!) tells us we can go no further.

The roadblock is full of Boomers and road trains waiting to get through. It's late afternoon so I turn directly east and ride someway into the desert where I can see evidence of mining. My intent is to make camp here, eat and get some rest before hopefully continuing south. I've been told the road may close again at 0630 so I'm not going to wait and leave before dawn.

As it turns out this is a very interesting place and somewhat risky as there are several deep shafts with their accompanying piles of spoil. I walk over to them and drop in a few flint boulders I find lying around; they are very deep. One has a cross and grave site. I know not of their origin, but I would think a fall in here would be fatal.

I amuse myself by practising a skill I learnt as a soldier, knapping flint, and make several very, very sharp blades. Further practice and I'll have made arrowheads like the original owners of this land, perfect for spearing, killing, gutting, skinning and butchering an animal. I make a short video of the skill.

Way off the highway I can be assured of a peaceful goodnight. I cook up some chorizo with beans and eat some smoked oysters and a little chocolate. It's very windy and dust is everywhere, yet many annoying, pesky flies buzz in my ears and nostrils. Swag and mozzie net up, it's time to watch the sun go down and it's a pearler. Then I lie down and slowly drift off under the southern stars again.

DAY 50

I wake at about 0500. The wind is howling, dust is everywhere, and the temperature seems close to zero – cold enough to freeze the balls off this brass monkey! I drop the swag and net and get going before 'Crab Air' starts dropping bombs again.

A little dodgy riding in the dark, but it's necessary. I'm very cold, not like caving in North Yorkshire cold, but the wind chill cuts through the clothing I'm wearing. After about three quarters of an hour of riding and singing stupid songs to keep up morale, I see the sun rise to my left and a layby appears on my right. It's time to pull in and get the billy on for hot coffee and hot food.

The gale continues to cut like a knife. I find a little respite, huddling down to avoid further wind-chill behind two busted up old dumpsters. The stove is also protected so hot water is on. It's difficult to avoid the wind when standing, so I look for a seat of some description. A short distance away is a discarded port-a-loo full of poo, so I get behind the protective box of steel.

Now I can sit down to cook and eat out of most of the chilling blow. It does 'pen and ink' a little, but necessity is the mother of invention. As I'm sitting there eating, watching crows pick the eyes out of a dead kangaroo and feeling the dusty wind bite behind two old dumpsters, it makes me think of a post-apocalyptic scene from *Mad Max* or something similar. Then the smell snaps me out of it, and I think of our Happy Clapper PM, Scott Morrison, and it came to me in a flash. How good is Australia!

Once fed and watered, I decide it's a good time to put on the DriRider wind and waterproofs. All good outdoors people know wind-proofing is important; that's why people live in little aluminium boxes on wheels out here. I then get my leg over. Peggy does not mind despite the icy draft.

On to Glendambo, the only roadhouse for 260 kilometres. The windproofs really help and before I know it an oasis of caffeine has arrived – GLENDAMBO! The name sounds like something out of a spaghetti western. We meet a family there, three boys and their parents, and they are curious about my faithful steed. I make the boys balloon swords, for which they are very happy.

Back on the road, Peggy and I have a race with a goods train on the Ghan line. It's easily a kilometre long and is beating us, frustrating Peggy; sometimes she forgets she's just a little green Army bike and thinks she is a BMW S1000RR with Barry Sheen on board (sometimes I think I'm Bazza). Just before the jump up to Woomera we pass Lake Hart, one of central Australia's big salt lakes. The vista is truly incredible: a shimmering white tablecloth lays over the landscape like it was thrown there by an Indigenous giant. I am captivated, especially when that same goods train rolls past its foreshore.

We are now at Spud's Roadhouse near Woomera, famous for its role in rocket launches and development. We will rest here tonight, tomorrow visit the base here and its myriad of historic aircraft, and then it's the final leg of the red centre to Port Augusta and a last turn east to the outback town of Broken Hill.

DAY 51

This morning is typified by two words, windy and dusty. The tent is rattling as a huge northerly blowing from the red interior blasts our camp near Woomera. Not a pleasant lie-in, so I drop the camp and make for coffee in Spud's Roadhouse. The staff here are very polite and helpful, and soon I'm eating and drinking a healthy breakfast.

We go to the rocket base to photograph the eclectic array of airplanes and rockets. Standouts for me were:

- The Gloster Meteor, one of Britain's first post war jet fighters.
- The Canberra medium range bomber, a very effective airplane right through the cold war and my youth.
- A rapier air defence missile system, our saviour during the Falklands war, defending British ships and planes from Argentine Skyhawk attacks that proved so crucial in the defence and eventual victory of British Forces.

- A Bofors anti-aircraft gun, known for firing flak rounds at enemy aircraft in WW2.
- Finally, a Thunderbird missile.

My last memory of these is asking my dad as a seven-year-old, "Why are all those rockets alongside the road dad?" His reply was, "They are all pointing at Russia, son."

That was at RAF Carnaby, East Yorkshire, during the Bay of Pigs crisis. We nearly had an all-out thermonuclear war, the closest we have been. Even as a young boy I remember the pervasive fear everywhere, even TV telling us to turn and drop, don't watch the flash!

Today's ride is south to Port Augusta, South Australia. While fuelling up, Peggy and I bump into four exhausted riders going north. They inform me the wind is a fight all the way. It's not long before I find out what they mean, fighting the handlebars and riding with a leftwards lean as the gale tries to push us into oncoming traffic.

With strong northerlies like this, often the dust of the Red Centre gets picked up and blown south to Adelaide, millions of tons of it. Today is one such day. I'm eating and breathing gritty saliva and air, as is Peggy. I try to snap a picture demonstrating the weather event, but it isn't very clear.

The Red Centre seems like it wants to hold onto you all the way across this vast continent, then suddenly you hit the Spencer Gulf and Southern Ocean at Port Augusta. I don't want to spend a great deal of time here. The dust is bad, and I find the place unpleasant. We look for the town's war memorials, of which it has two, one for north of the estuary and one for the south. During WW1, the two places were separated, but now there is a bridge.

Leaving the port, we stop for refreshments and are immediately enthusiastically set upon by two beautiful children. They say, "Thank you for your service." I look behind me, but they are talking to Peggy and me. Mum wants photos so we happily oblige and speak for several minutes before we ride away.

Heading down the eastern side of the Spencer Gulf, we quickly reach the turn off for Wilmington and the brilliant Horrocks Pass, up through verdant rolling hills with formations and high ground resembling the face of a steam iron. It's a great twisting switchback pass up the range that is great fun on any motorcycle. If I lived in Port Augusta, I would be here often on my S1000RR Beemer.

We stop at the quaint village of Wilmington to look at the Land Rover display and have a quick ale in the great period pub. Leaving the town is windy but through pleasant fertile farming land. There are many fields of wheat and other crops turning gold in the early Australian spring.

Eventually we end up in the South Australian locality of Peterborough, a town with a motorcycle museum. Peterborough is the steam rail town that time forgot; what a jewel this place is. It has the longest, prettiest main street I have seen this trip. Lined with old buildings from another time, a rail line running parallel to it, even the kerbstones and footpaths smack of the early 20th century, with slate slabs and big sandstone kerb stones thirty centimetres high. The town was once Steam Railway Central in Australia, boasting all three gauges of line, and a hub where thousands of steam trains came to be serviced and repaired at the Roundhouse specially built for the purpose.

The sense that the townspeople are proud, and its leaders take care to preserve history is strong. I stay at the historic Peterborough Hotel, my fourth real bed on this two-month trip. It's a very motorcycle friendly pub and the owner Neil is a keen rider himself. Great food, cold beer and a very friendly atmosphere with lock up parking for bikes – Peggy is very happy. I shower and get the dust out of places you don't want to know about. Tomorrow we head east to the outback town of Broken Hill.

DAY 52

The Good, the Bad and the Ugly meets Mad Max:

THE GOOD

I sleep really well only waking as the rays of light come through the curtains. I go for another shower and it's sheer bliss to be this clean! I pack up our things, load Peggy and look for some breakfast and coffee on the mega-long high street.

Happily refreshed and no longer pining for the fjords, I brush down my plumage, jump on Peggy, start her thumper and ride off north-east. Leaving the emerald paddocks of this agricultural region, we're heading for Broken Hill and my home state of NSW.

THE BAD

It's not long before the north-easterly winds pick up to gale force again, threatening to blow the tank bag in my face. The landscape changes back to dry desert, with undulating hills surrounding the horizon on all sides. The road looks like a glistening black snake winding its way to the vanishing point over the hills. The dust storm that accompanies the wind is choking. I can taste soil and dirt; Peggy's air filter will be clogged. All this dust will end up in Sydney and other cities. We pass through several ghost towns with wind-torn wooden ruins, doors and windows swinging wildly. At any moment Clint Eastwood will step out, cigar gripped in his teeth and point his colt revolver at us. I stop and try to photograph the gritty haze, but again the camera will not do the unpleasant experience justice.

THE UGLY

As we reach the NSW border the scenery becomes terribly desolate. Dry, barren, rocky ground lines both sides of the highway, looking akin to a nuclear wasteland. That's why they filmed *Mad Max* in this region – nothing could be more convincing of atomic devastation than here with Silverton just up the road, where most of this seminal film was first made. On arrival at Broken Hill, the first thing you see is a massive solar farm and wind farm to the north. I would not like the job of cleaning dust off those panels! Next to my left is the biggest cemetery I have ever seen. Either they can't get the dead out of town, or the crematorium is out of gas.

When we arrive in Broken Hill proper, my initial reaction is one of dislike, but this mining town is a paradox in the desert. We are sitting in a club at the moment, washing dust from my throat and contemplating getting to grips with this mining town. Further inspection reveals a vibrant community with lovely architecture and friendly folk.

Broken Hill is a town that is literally built around a broken hill containing the biggest ore body of silver, zinc and lead in the world. The deposit is 1.8 million years old, shaped like a boomerang and buried in the earth's crust, apex uppermost and wings descending to great depth. Lead pollution is a huge problem here. All children have their blood lead levels checked frequently, so many clean up campaigns have been enacted by governments. Peggy and I explore and find the war memorial, a very well-built structure worthy of the diggers who sacrificed it all.

The weather is about to change. The cold front that brought so much wind and dust now heralds wet weather. Peggy and I find a camp at the base of a massive mining structure just outside town. After dinner we retire there and for the first time in many weeks set up a tent, batten down the hatches and wait for the event to pass through. As is typical of these fronts in Australia, it goes through quickly during the night leaving little rain, but we do get a splash.

DAY 53

Morning and everything is damp. A few drops of condensation wakes me, dribbling across my face. Up and at 'em! Despite wanting to get home and see my puppies today, I want to visit Silverton and make a 300 kilometre detour to Menindee Lakes, the site of devastating fish kills this year and extreme water shortage. With the advent of false news – the ultimate cop out for lying politicians – I wanted to find out for myself, meet the locals and see the results of another man-made disaster.

Striking camp, and everything is wet! Breakfast and coffee are next on my agenda, so into town we go. After sustenance, Peggy and I are off north to Silverton. The country is amorphous, arid and featureless. At any moment I expect to be overtaken by a handsome young man wearing black leathers, sporting a sawn-off shotgun and driving a Black Ford Falcon with a supercharger protruding through the bonnet! You guessed it – *Mad Max* country and it looks every bit of the landscape in that epic movie. Nothing here but sand, scrub and straight narrow roads.

Arriving in Silverton the first thing that strikes hard is the frontier look of the place, dirt roads through town, and old western style buildings. I half expect to see Yul Brynner tying up a horse and removing his gun belt. As we approach the Silverton Hotel a persistent kelpie thinks Peggy needs rounding up and counters my every move to avoid her directions. The hotel is a period piece both inside and out. I step into the 1800s badlands. Two donkeys outside add to the atmosphere.

As I am hanging around outside drinking yet more coffee, a young gent arrives on his lovely black Ducati Diavil. He is interested in our story, so we get chatting. Turns out he is a farmer from Swan Hill, south of here. He was having a mental health day on his sickle, times are tough for him, with drought, climate change and water politics pushing him and many other farmers near the edge. He is not optimistic about the future, but he's a really nice, honest fella and we make a promise to keep in touch.

Menindee lies 140 kilometres south of here and I am anxious to see the truth for myself. Without further ado Peggy and I are off, back through Broken Hill and due south through now familiar barren terrain for a couple of hours. I keep a wary eye for wildlife especially kangaroos and sporadic sheep as they are very apt at jumping into my path. There are loads of carcasses in evidence of that behaviour. Looking to the horizon, I see nothing but desert and spinifex.

When we arrive in Menindee, we ride straight to the Menindee Lake Lookout. There is no lake! This massive water feature is gone, leaving a few dead trees and a flat sandy bottom to mark its passing. How very sad such a thing has been lost, albeit temporarily. We ride on into town and the broken heart of this riverside community. There is no water here. They depend on donations from Adelaide and others. Some townsfolk have drilled bores, but the government in its wisdom refuses to accept any liability for any toxic water the bores may produce. This community has been left on its own and government has washed their hands, excuse the pun!

Stopping at a little cafe on the corner of the main street I meet and chat with three lovely local ladies, all of whom have lived here over many years. I'm curious about their water supply and in particular Menindee Lakes. They are all emphatic stating their position.

"Successive governments have drained and pumped the lakes dry several times in the last sixteen years."

"Why?" I ask.

"To fill the irrigation reservoirs of cotton growers and the massive almond farms to the east!

All this environmental vandalism so politicians can satisfy the greed of their big business mates and so yuppies in Melbourne, Brisbane, Perth and Sydney can have almond milk in their lattes whilst sitting in the waiting room, ready for their next Botox injections. Let's not mention the cotton that goes to China and gets sold back to those same yuppies as a cheap t-shirt to wear once to a trendy night club and never again. There, I said it! We are a carelessly materialistic and self-centred society.

Those are some of the facts emphasised with a little rhetorical metaphor for shits and giggles, and there is little to giggle about in the Murray Darling Basin.

The girls say, "Go and look at the bit of the river we have left!" The water's all gone further up and down stream, but they direct Peggy and me only 500 metres down the road. When we arrive, we are greeted by a smelly, green, toxic stretch of water in which millions of fish have died recently. Make no mistake, this is dead, poisonous H2O – nothing survives in its hypoxic depths except for blue-green algae.

A local grandad pulls up with his two little grandsons to look. The boys asked if they could approach the water's edge. "No!" said the grandfather, emphatically, "If you fall in, you will be very sick." By this time I am very sad, enough is enough. I had wanted to see the truth and it hurts.

A region raped, pillaged and set adrift by the likes of Barnaby Joyce. The locals tell me that before the election our leaders were tripping over each other in this place, anxious to be seen and heard, and calling for a Royal Commission. Victory to the LNP and nothing has been heard since. These are the 'honourable men' that exist in today's parliaments but in reality it is an apolitical issue that spans many decades and governments.

I have seen more than I desired and fortunately I can leave which I do, following the multi-billion-dollar pipeline that had to be built supplying the mines and city of Broken Hill over two hundred kilometres away. Some needs are greater than others, eh?

The ride towards home is much of the same and uneventful. I take one final picture today of the Palace Hotel, the scene of some shenanigans in that hilarious and adorable movie, *Priscilla Queen of the Desert*. Late in the evening, Peggy and I leave Broken Hill on the road south to Mildura, Victoria, some 300 kilometres. Once clear of Broken Hill by about thirty kilometres, we start looking for a camp for the night as light is fading. We find a gravel pit at the roadside and hide ourselves away behind the piles of road gravel. It's a little chilly as the sun sets to the west and the odd car and road train passes by. All in all, though, it's a good little spot to sleep the night.

Setting camp does not take long. I am well-rehearsed now. I lie down and think of home and seeing my dogs again, especially Loretta. Before long I am in the land of nod.

DAY 54

I wake really early at 0300 and it's cold. My old APTC, Army and adventure scars are aching, especially my back and shoulders. I toss and turn until about 0500, when I can see the sun starting to rise out the tent door, which I always face east when setting camp. It's an old but simple trick that makes you feel slightly better as the sun starts to warm the tent door, and good for morale. There's no point in lying there so I get up and the billy goes on for morning coffee. I relax a little drinking the warm sweet brew and make mental plans for the day, to reach Mildura down The Silver Town Highway.

Striking camp is a doddle; everything's nice and dry. It's a cold morning though, so I wrap up well, kick Peggy in the guts and despite the cold she fires up the first time as always. Onto the road we go. The wind chill is bad, so after some time I stop and put on my windproofs, something I should have done earlier.

The highway itself is not remarkable. It's flat, barren, dry and straight. It does, however, have the pipeline feeding Broken Hill with its water from the Murray River at Mildura 300 kilometres south. I have been told to look out for this and in the morning light it becomes clear.

The entire right-hand side of the road is a massive scar where the pipeline was laid. Truly, thousands and thousands of native trees and vegetation have been bulldozed to facilitate the pumping of water to Broken Hill. The landscape is wounded, vandalised by careless governments who have squandered water at Menindee Lakes irrigating massive cotton, almond and rice farms further upstream. Basically the water in Menindee Lakes that kept taps flowing in Broken Hill for decades was sold and now it's gone. Therefore a pipeline to give life to Broken Hill was built, taking water from further down the now dead system. How's that for robbing Peter to pay Paul!

And Gina Reinhart now wants to tap into the Fitzroy River in the Kimberley so she can sell Aussie milk to China. Let's hope this never happens to another of Australia's magnificent river systems.

It's a long ride this morning so I take a break at a layby. Strangely there are signs saying,

ENVIRONMENTALLY FRAGILE AREA. PLEASE KEEP OUT

and

SIGNIFICANT NATIVE VEGETATION

They are there to keep people from walking on the area adjacent. Not even fifty metres across the road, however, the government has created a completely dead zone. Nothing but bulldozed timber for hundreds of kilometres.

Who are these fools? These Hollow Men and Women, and how do they reach their positions and pay grades? An older lady, stopped in her car, points it out to me again, shrugs her shoulders and says, "Everyone knows it's a crime born of power and money."

The day's warming up now, and after another 160 kilometres or so I will be in Mildura. I throw my leg over Peggy and press her starter, and we're off. It does not seem that long before we arrive in Wentworth, NSW. Time to fuel up Peggy and get me a sausage roll and coffee. We leave Wentworth for Mildura, only thirty kilometres away, and cross the Murray River into Victoria. This region is a big producer of wine, and vineyards line the roads in long rows like soldiers on parade.

Peggy and I arrive in Mildura in the afternoon, and after a quick ale we search out Super Cheap Auto. Not for car parts but for some metal putty. I've broken my specs again! This stuff is magic – a quick knead into putty and mould into place, and specs are as good as new.

With good vision restored, we think we would take a bite out of the over 500 kilometre journey facing us, back on the road east to Wagga Wagga. Shortly after leaving, I'm riding Peggy visor up when suddenly a large bee flies into my helmet.

I know I'm going to get stung, and the airborne arthropod goes straight around my head and stings me on the temple. The pain is not that bad really; just the feeling of a little creepy-crawly working its way around my face – *arggggh*! But if you could see me pulling off the road, trying to remove gloves, struggling to undo the strap and get the specs and helmet off, you would laugh. It must look hilarious!

I never find the little twat. After a thorough inspection of my helmet I put it on again and resume the ride. I've intended to get to a place called Euston, and I'm so glad we get there. There's a great little pub, nice people and excellent tucker by a glowing log fire. After dinner, I find a perfect camp spot right by the Murray River. I set up the tent and retire at about 2000 hours.

DAY 55

Waking in the morning at 0600, I rip into striking camp and go for breakfast and a clean up in the local public toilet. I have a weather window. If I can get home by Wednesday, I will miss the next cold front. I notice mares' tails or cirrus clouds, a clear indication of a rapidly approaching cold front. No more messing around, no more visiting interesting local features, and Peggy's back tyre has had it anyway.

I ride long and hard to get to Wagga Wagga this evening, striking distance to Canberra and my friends, Ken and Fran. First, we stop for a quick coffee and photo of the war memorial in Balranald, a small town on the way to Hay NSW. Despite the weather urgency, Peggy and I try to visit every town's memorial to commemorate and honour our fallen heroes.

Next the Hay Plains, flat and dry much like the whole region. I do notice many high levy banks at the roadside, so I stop to see what was on the other side: nothing, not a skerrick of water, but they must have been full once. I stop in Hay for lunch at a local cafe. It's the same old story from the owner. Water squandered by governments, leaving the town struggling in the big dry. I eat some fish for lunch, pay my respects at the town war memorial, then start the long ride to Wagga Wagga.

Much of the same parched, once fertile now barren, agricultural landscape borders the road. We reach another NSW Riverina town called Narrandera, search out the memorial and take more pictures. Then into the pub for a quick middy and chat with locals. Everyone you speak to seems worried about the water situation. Local men who work at a rice farm told me their jobs will go next year as the water allocations have been removed. Rice is a very water dependent crop, but at least you can eat it.

Back on Peggy, with less than a hundred kilometres to Wagga Wagga. A tail wind has been pushing us all day, so Peggy has been performing like a sports bike! Well, perhaps not – but never let the truth stand in the way of a good story.

We are now twenty kilometres outside Wagga Wagga at the pub in Collingullie, NSW. Our penultimate night of this two-month mission is spent in the Gullie Hotel. A good meal, a couple of ales and a warm soft bed is just the ticket. Fed, showered and watered, an early night as usual with Peggy just outside the door.

DAY 56

We wake to a very frosty morning, and another shower to warm up. Dressed and packed, we are soon on our way to Canberra. Leaving through Wagga reminds me why I live in a remote village in south-east NSW. So many cars, trucks, traffic lights and impatient people, but we do get through unscathed. Once clear of Wagga the country soon becomes the familiar green rolling paddocks of my home, a contrast to the russet, arid and rocky land-scapes now in our wake. I can breathe easy on the home run.

It's not long until we reached Gundagai, home of the famous Dog on the Tucker Box now restored after recent vandalism. The monument stands in tribute to dogs that reputedly guarded their owners' tucker box whilst they were away working the bull-ock teams. Legend has it that one canine remained with his master's tucker box faithfully waiting for his master's return; he was not to return – he had died. The story has been put into the folklore of modern Australian history. After getting pics, coffee and carrot cake, Peggy and I leave for the remaining uneventful drive on the freeway to Canberra. Once in the nation's capital and on Northbourne Avenue, we notice the newly built tram lines down the centre, a little cosmopolitan addition of a mass transport system.

It's Peggy who asks me if we could visit Anzac parade and get a photo of her by all the memorials lining the road to the Australian War Memorial, so we do. It should be remembered each structure is not celebrating war, it is commemorating the loss of lives in each conflict. Now I can say this because my brothers and sisters and I have all at some stage put ourselves in harm's way and risked it all for our country and others; that's a fact.

Our war dead did not 'give up' their lives. The fact is their lives were often stolen by fat old men in suits smoking cigars and the wars they started, conscription and the use of jingoistic rhetoric, ensured young men and women were sent into the breach and to their deaths. We must never forget the histories of these youngsters. Unfortunately we will continue to build more memorials, because even as I type our PM and POTUS are fuelling the fires of yet another conflict. Syria, Yemen, Papua are not enough for the economics of death and killing babies with bombs made in Australia.

Lest We Forget all my friends, sisters and brothers wounded physically and mentally by such evil men and women.

Duty done by Peggy and me, we fall out of the Parade on Anzac Avenue. Peggy wants to see Parliament House, so we ride up the main ramp and stop for a picture of the place that now has a high steel fence and permanently circling police vehicles protecting the cowards who sit inside making unjust laws. We have seen for ourselves the results of their decisions on First Australians in the Far North and the devastation of water supplies in the Murray Darling Basin.

We are immediately moved on, as there's to be no stopping for photos.

A short while later we arrived at Ken and Fran's place where our last night on the road will be spent. Slow cooked lamb shanks in red wine for dinner apparently, one of my favourite meals.

Tomorrow is the final day. 200 kilometres to my simple, environmentally friendly home in the mountains, Anthony the house-sitter and good mate, a nice curry dinner and a play with my puppies. This mission has been a greater success than I could have imagined.

DAY 57

The ride back home is one I do many times a year, south on the Monaro Highway via Cooma, NSW. I am very excited by the prospect of seeing my dogs and friends again. I do stop to let Anthony know I am close so as he can bring the dogs to my gate and greet me. After the two-hour ride, Peggy and I get home. Loretta, my little whippet pup, goes crazy to see me. She has not forgotten me.

Time to relax and let myself absorb the experiences of my long travels.

EVALUATION AND CONCLUSIONS

1. To deliver First Aid and basic care to remote communities.

During our first big lap of Australia, I was shocked by the numbers of wounds and easily treated conditions such as eye and skin infections that I witnessed. On this occasion I was pleased to see a lot less of this sort of thing. Whether coincidence or not, the number of people wandering about with injuries or conditions was down, and our first aid service was not needed quite as much as it may have been in 2018. Recent media reports have highlighted the issues facing First Australians; this hopefully could be one reason.

We did treat many minor wounds and give out dressings etc to people. Also, soothing eye drops were in great demand, and I was administering and handing them out as required. Anti-fungal creams were also used and handed out.

The fact minor injuries seemed less common was a good thing and of course I was pleased; however, the extent of major physical disease, mental illness and trauma had not changed. First Australians are still dying much younger than their white or European counterparts. Obvious diseases and conditions such as leprosy, diabetic complications and amputations, mental illness, suicide, congenital syphilis and foetal alcohol syndrome were all present in remote communities of the Kimberley.

More worrying to me was the amount of serious dental disease I witnessed. Most adults had some level of decay and in many the condition was extreme. Lack of education, hygiene and any treatment are a root cause. Dental disease is a precursor to many other life-threatening illnesses, like heart disease, stroke, meningitis. Of course, dental decay is not restricted to Indigenous groups and is found elsewhere, but not to the extent I saw. The seriousness of the decay was the worst I've seen in my career.

In addition, the endemic nature of trachoma (caused by the bacterium chlamydia trachomatis resulting in an infection of the eye) in Australia is something we should be ashamed of; we are the last developed nation on the planet to still have this easily cured disease in our population.

The fact the Kimberley has the highest suicide rate in the world is not lost on me. I saw such loss of hope and talk of suicide, people dispossessed, people discriminated against by governments and agencies such as the police, local councils and white Australians. Also, so many people are homeless.

With no support structures they wander the streets, some obviously psychotic and confused. Little if anything is being done to address this issue.

2. *To document and make photographic and other records of the social and health disadvantages and diseases we encounter.*

Cultural and personal differences meant making photographic records difficult, but the verbal accounts and witnessing of such deprivations firsthand facilitated this goal to a greater extent than I could have imagined. Peggy and I were readily accepted into the open Indigenous communities we visited. I spoke at length with Elders and many others about their lives, illnesses and historical abuse they had endured.

First Australians have a long oral history and collective memory passed down through the generations. Many are angry and feel forgotten by mainstream Australia. Some of the abuses they suffered were obscene and within living memory. Massacres, murders, rapes and Stolen Generations went on right through the 20th century and some more subtle crimes continue to this day. Some Elders I spoke with believe the deprivation, discrimination and disease they live with is an unspoken slow genocide, and future generations and culture will be lost.

3. *To bring these records back and make them available to the media, politicians and the general community.*

Exceeding all my expectations, my daily blog, meetings with Elders, and my own experiences have resulted in a comprehensive record forming the skeleton of this book. In addition to that, the #murielthemedicycle web page has had 60,000 interactions and hits. I never expected such a response; each post reached between 3000 to 5000 people and on one occasion a boosted post reached 17,000.

4. *To deliver simple health and hygiene education to the communities we visit.*

Many of the communities and people I met found English and particularly my accent difficult. Unfortunately I rarely had enough people in one place to discuss health and hygiene in detail. I did give advice on an individual basis as I travelled and worked, especially to parents. There are several campaigns being conducted in the Indigenous community addressing STDs, trachoma, and hygiene, but they don't seem to be very effective as they bear little relevance or cultural sensitivity to the Indigenous people or their language and customs.

5. *To provide some simple recreation programs in communities we visit.*

Well, I never! When my planning team suggested I conduct some recreation programs I was sceptical. Balloon modelling, a simple idea, was extremely successful. Wherever we went and met with hundreds of local Indigenous children, Mr Balloon came out and was immediately surrounded by excited children. It was a touch of sheer genius by my team to suggest this. If I were to conduct another trip, I would probably make it a clowning or magician format.

Some white Australians and officials seemed challenged by the amount of joy this was giving, viewing the numbers of happy children with suspicion and discriminatory comments. On some occasions I was made to feel threatened or suspect.

6. *Unexpected outcomes of inappropriate water use, theft and drought.*

When I set out on this long difficult odyssey, I had many fears and reservations concerning the success and acceptance of our help by Indigenous communities. Never in my wildest dreams did I expect to find yet another group of people who had been devastated by successive government incompetence and corruption.

During my travels across Northern Queensland, New South Wales and particularly the Murray Darling Basin, I was shocked by the gross mismanagement of our biggest water resource. I saw for myself what I had only heard about on the news. I spoke with people living in these arid communities, and I was told of the sale of precious water to industries such as cotton farming, almond farming, and rice farming. The state of the rivers was appalling; many were just stinking pools of stagnant, toxic water with dead fish and birds.

Seeing such waste, greed and its effect on communities that politicians see as expendable made me very sad and angry. There is so little anyone can do when ministers seem to be in the pocket of big business and sell out the people.

We must remain vigilant and be activists, for even now people like Gina Reinhart are planning to irrigate dairy farms in the Kimberley using precious water from the Fitzroy River in Western Australia. This must not be allowed to happen. These water allocations and sales serve only to make already obscenely wealthy business people and politicians even richer; how much money do they need? The Adani mine is another example, threatening the Great Artesian Basin and the people who depend on it are living in fear. All these business schemes and plans are not being made with the needs of First Australians in mind, more the needs of millionaires and their political allies. Little benefit will reach locals, but they will have to deal with their lands – their cultural identities – being taken and trashed.

EVALUATION

On all of the parameters and goals we set, the program was a great success. We achieved all our goals, and some exceeded my expectations. The level of awareness and interaction we created in the community was much higher than I anticipated. Much of this success was undoubtedly a result of the daily blog I wrote and the personification of Peggy, my little motorbike. I cannot overstate the success of using her again this year. Peggy broke the ice in communities, as people were interested in her story.

Whilst the amount of First Aid treatment required was down on last year, that can't be regarded as a lack of success, yet it's a very positive outcome. The prospect of this book continues the great work we started.

CONCLUSIONS AND RECOMMENDATIONS

There remains a great need in the Indigenous communities of the far north, for their health and lifespan are much lower than the general community. Discrimination and lack of opportunity are still strong in the minds of many. Further education for young Australians on the true history of 60,000 years of peoples who live on this vast continent would go a long way dispelling many myths. I thoroughly recommend the book *Dark Emu* by Bruce Pascoe to anyone who wants to understand Australia's First Nations' heritage.

First Australians will continue to suffer until successive governments stop their exploitation of Indigenous country for mining, fracking and water resources. The discrimination that allows for the gaps in life expectancy, health care and mental wellbeing must stop.

First Australians must feel they are important, they must have a voice, and perhaps including them in the Australian constitution, would be a start. The tokenism of representation also steals their power.

Throwing more money at the issues is not always the answer, and many of these people feel lost, disempowered, forgotten and hidden from mainstream society. These problems are the same wherever colonisation has occurred throughout the world. That is no coincidence.

Last Thoughts

After returning from my mission in October 2019, I was soon surrounded by massive bush fires that took the homes and lives of many in my region. As if that was not enough, we were then caught up in the Covid-19 pandemic, being locked down in our homes and subject to all manner of restrictions and fear-provoking media and government reports.

During the pandemic I found myself asking questions of myself in the quiet solitary moments. The paradox of what I had witnessed in First Nations communities was not lost on me. Two centuries ago, we whitefellas brought Smallpox, Syphilis, Leprosy and Influenza to this Great Southern Land. These epidemics wiped out millions, and despite being easily cured and treated they are still endemic in the Far North, while few of us whitefellas even know, and some don't care.

But now we have our own plague, our healthy happy bubble has been burst, we are now living in fear, we are now stressed by the instigations of laws, rules and some panic. State Governments, Federal Governments and politicians jostle for power and control. We are now the ones subject to the whims of others, we are now the ones being controlled and following orders of the system. How IRONIC can life be?

ACKNOWLEDGMENTS

Thanks must go to the individuals who helped with the planning and implementation of Muriel the Medicycle:

Col Roger Thayne RAMC rtd
Anthony Mims MIMZY
Anthony Urquhart
Isabel Robinson
Josh Safarti
Ken Purbrick
Fran Purbrick

CPSIA information can be obtained
at www.ICGtesting.com
Printed in the USA
BVHW052301301121
622870BV00003B/286

9 780645 163124